Edward McCrady

An Historic Church. The Westminster Abbey of South Carolina

A Sketch of St. Philips Church, Charleston, S. C.

Edward McCrady

An Historic Church. The Westminster Abbey of South Carolina
A Sketch of St. Philips Church, Charleston, S. C.

ISBN/EAN: 9783337161422

Printed in Europe, USA, Canada, Australia, Japan

Cover: Foto ©Lupo / pixelio.de

More available books at **www.hansebooks.com**

AN HISTORIC CHURCH.

THE WESTMINSTER ABBEY OF SOUTH CAROLINA.

A Sketch of

ST. PHILIP'S CHURCH,

CHARLESTON, S. C.,

FROM THE ESTABLISHMENT OF THE CHURCH OF ENGLAND UNDER
THE ROYAL CHARTER OF 1665 TO THE PRESENT TIME
(JULY, 1897).

BY

EDWARD McCRADY, SENIOR WARDEN.

CHARLESTON, S. C.
LUCAS & RICHARDSON CO., PRINTERS AND ENGRAVERS,
130 East Bay Street.
1897.

AN HISTORIC CHURCH. .

THE WESTMINSTER ABBEY OF SOUTH CAROLINA.

A Sketch of

ST. PHILIP'S CHURCH,

CHARLESTON, S. C.,

FROM THE ESTABLISHMENT OF THE CHURCH OF ENGLAND UNDER
THE ROYAL CHARTER OF 1665 TO THE PRESENT TIME
(JULY, 1897).

BY

EDWARD McCRADY, SENIOR WARDEN.

CHARLESTON, S. C.
LUCAS & RICHARDSON CO., PRINTERS AND ENGRAVERS.
130 East Bay Street.
1897.

Rector.

Rev. JOHN JOHNSON, D. D.

Wardens.

EDWARD McCRADY.   WILLIAM H. PRIOLEAU, M. D.

Vestrymen.

CHARLES. F. HANCKEL.   EDWARD M. MORELAND.
JOHN M. KINLOCH.   BARNWELL RHETT BURNET.
THOMAS S. SINKLER.   WALTER PRINGLE.

ISAAC MAZYCK.

Delegates to the Diocesan Council.

EDWARD McCRADY.   WILLIAM H. PRIOLEAU, M. D.
JOHN M. KINLOCH.   ISAAC MAZYCK.

Committee of Advice Parish Church Home.

H. W. DeSAUSSURE, M. D.   LOUIS deB. McCRADY.
THEODORE D. JERVEY.   J. NORTH SMITH.

R. HEBER SCREVEN.

Committee on Finance Parish Church Home.

CASPAR A. CHISOLM.   EDWARD M. MORELAND.
W. W. SHACKELFORD.   THOMAS W. BACOT.

GEORGE T. PRINGLE.

Solicitor.

THOMAS W. BACOT.

Secretary and Treasurer.

ARTHUR MAZYCK.

AN HISTORIC CHURCH.

THE WESTMINSTER ABBEY OF SOUTH CAROLINA.

A Sketch of St. Philip's Church, Charleston, S. C., from the Establishment of the Church of England, under the Royal Charter of 1665, to the Present Time.

By EDWARD McCRADY, Senior Warden.

The early history of St. Philip's Church is but a part of the colonial history of South Carolina ; and as it has been said of Westminster Abbey that it was a part of the Constitution of England, so St. Philip's was interwoven into the very fabric of the Province.

The charter of King Charles II, (1665), under which the colony was founded, granted unto the Lords Proprietors "the patronage and advowsons of all the churches and chappels" (i. e. the power to name and appoint ministers) "which as the Christian religion shall increase within the Province, territory, islets and limits aforesaid, shall happen hereafter to be erected ; together with license and power to build and found churches, chappels and oratories in convenient and fit places within the said bounds and limits, and to cause them to be dedicated and consecrated according to the ecclesiastical laws of our Kingdom of England."

In pursuance of this provision of their charter, the Proprietors in the famous Fundamental Constitutions, which they endeavored to impose, inserted the following clause :

" As the country comes to be sufficiently planted, and distributed into fit divisions, it shall belong to the Parliament to take care for the building of churches and the public maintenance of divines, to be employed in the exercise of religion, according to the Church of England; which being the only true and orthodox, and the national religion of all the King's dominions, is so also of Carolina; and therefore it alone shall be allowed to receive public maintenance by grant of Parliament."

These Fundamental Constitutions, as they were termed, were never assented to by the people of the Province, and so were never constitutionally in force under the charter. But the Church of England was accepted by the colonists as established under the charter. And so we find Governor Sayle, Puritan though he himself was said to have been, writing to the Proprietors within three months after the arrival of the colony on the Ashley (25 June, 1670,) that a clergyman of the Church of England should be sent to them—"one Mr. Sampson Bond, heretofore of long standing in Exeter College in Oxford, and ordaigned by the late Bishop of Exeter, the ole Do'r Joseph Hall." And again in a letter of 9th September, in which Forence O'Sullivan, Stephen Bull, Joseph West, Ralph Marshall, Paul Smith, Samuel West and Joseph Dalton unite, he urges the want of an able minister by whose means corrupted youth might be reclaimed, and the people instructed. "The Israelites' prosperity decayed when their prophets were wanting, for where the ark of God is," he says, "there is peace and tranquility." [*Calendar State Papers Colonial (Sainsbury) London, 1889, 202-246.*] The Rev. Mr. Bond, who was in Bermuda, did not come, though the Proprietors offered him 500 acres of land and £40 per annum if he would do so.

It is not known certainly when the first minister came into the Province. The Rev. Dr. Dalcho heads the list of the clergy in South Carolina with the name of Morgan Jones as being in the Province in 1660; and Bishop Perry in his *History of the American Episcopal Church (Vol. 1, 372,)* gives a letter which first appeared in the *Gentleman's Magazine for March, 1740, (Vol. 10, 103-4)* purporting to have been written by this clergyman March 10, 1685-6, in which he states that he was sent from Virginia by Sir

William Berkeley, the Governor, to meet the fleet under West on its arrival. The letter is full of anachronisms and impossibilities, and is manifestly a fabrication. It is safe to say that no such clergyman was in the Province at that time; indeed there was no Province of Carolina in 1660.

We have no account of the building of any church in Old Town, on the Ashley, the site occupied by the colonists for the first ten years after their arrival in Carolina. Culpepper, the Surveyor General in 1772, marks a tract reserved, as he supposed, for a minister. Bishop Perry in his *History of the American Episcopal Church, Vol. I, 372*, quotes a letter of Commissary Johnson, written in 1710, in which he states that the Rev. Atkin Williamson had been in the Province 29 years, which would imply his arrival in 1681. But in a deed of Originall Jackson and Meliscent, his wife, giving a tract of land for another church, dated January 14, 1680-1, Mr. Williamson is mentioned as then officiating. The inference is, therefore, that he had arrived at least as early as some time in 1680. Mr. Williamson in 1709 petitioned the General Assembly "to be considered for his services in officiating as minister of Charles Town," and the Act of 1710, appropriating £30 per annum to his support, states "that he had grown so disabled with age, sickness and other infirmities that he could no longer attend to the duties of his ministerial functions, and was so poor that he could not maintain himself." (*Dalcho's Church Hist., 32.*) There was a clergyman in Carolina in 1689, for it was one of the tyranical acts of Governor Colleton that he fined and imprisoned him for preaching what the Governor considered a seditious sermon. (*Hist. Sketches of So. Ca., Rivers, 410.*) But who this minister was, Mr. Williamson or another, is not known. Mr. Williamson was certainly in the Province at that time.

Neither is it certainly known when the first church-building was erected within the limits of the present city. We do know pretty conclusively that no such building had been erected in 1682. For Thomas Ash, a clerk on board the Richmond, the vessel that brought the first Huguenots in

1680, in a description of Carolina published upon his return in 1682, says: "The town is regularly laid out into large and capacious streets, which to buildings is a great ornament and beauty. *In it they have reserved convenient places for a church, town house and other public structures.*" (*Carrol's Collection, Vol. 2, 82.*) We may safely assume that no church had then been built, for the writer, who was so particular in saying that a place had been reserved for a church, would certainly have mentioned it, had one then been built. The site reserved for the church is that at the southeast corner of what are now Broad and Meeting Streets, and upon it was erected the first St. Philip's Church, where now stands St. Michael's. So this spot, set apart at the very inception of the city, has remained until this day consecrated to the service of God and separated from all unhallowed, worldly and common uses. The plot reserved was not, however, nearly as large as that occupied by the present Church of St. Michael's and its grave yard. It was not much deeper upon Broad Street than the length of the present church. This we know because by a deed dated June 11, 1697, a lot of land adjoining the church was conveyed "to the Right Honorable Proprietor Joseph Blake, Governor, and his successors in trust for the use of St. Philip's Church for a yard thereunto forever." (*Dalcho's Church History, 27.*) The dimensions of this lot thus added are not given. But again in 1816 another lot was purchased and added to the church yard which was forty feet in depth, extending from the present Mansion House so as to include the iron gate that opens on Broad Street, which leaves but thirty feet between the gate and the church for the lot conveyed to Governor Blake as an addition to the original church yard. "The Octogenerian Lady," who wrote in 1855, tells us that "the city square was originally the grave yard of the first St. Philip's or English Church, which was built on the spot where the only St. Michael's stands." But for this we have no other authority. The Church was first known as "the Church" or "the English Church." Its distinctive name "St. Philip's" first appears in the deed to Governor Blake in 1697, above referred to. Ramsay states that the first church was built about 1690, but gives no authority. Dr. Dalcho thinks that it was built in 1681 or 1682. As we have said, we may assume that it had not been built in 1682 ; but probably it was built before 1690. This is all that can be said on the subject. Whenever built, it was of black cypress upon a brick foundation, and was said to have been "large and stately." It was surrounded by a neat white palisade fence. It must, however, have been very hastily built and of unseasoned materials as the Act of 1720 for hastening the completion of the new brick church which had been begun in 1710 recites that it "must inevitably in a very little time fall to the ground, the timbers being rotten and the whole fabric entirely decayed." This may be added to Dr. Dalcho's reasons for fixing the earlier date of its erection.

Though Mr. Williamson was still officiating in the colony he does not appear to have been the minister of St. Philip's in 1696, for Dalcho states that that year, the Church being vacant, the Rev Samuel Marshall, A. M., was appointed to the cure. Mr. Marshall came out recommended by the Lord Bishop of London and the Lords Proprietors of the Province as a sober, worthy, able and learned divine, a recommendation of which the Act of 1698, settling a maintenance on a minister of the Church of England in Charles Town, declares by his devout and exemplary life and good doctrine he had approved himself worthy. His rectorship was, however, short ; he died of yellow fever in 1699, the first appearance of that malignant disease in the Province.

Two events of great interest to the Church took place in the year 1698, during Mr. Marshall's brief ministry, the first of which was the passage of "*An Act to settle a maintenance on a minister of the Church of England in Charles Town*." From the recital in this Act we learn that Mr. Marshall, "out of the zeal he had for the propagation of the Christian religion, and particularly that of the Church of England," had "left a considerable benefice and honorable way of living in England to come out to Carolina," and for that

reason, and upon the recommendation of the Bishop of
London and the Lords Proprietors, the Act provided that he
should enjoy all the lands, houses, negroes, cattle and
moneys appointed for the use, benefit and behoof of the
minister of Charles Town, and specifically appropriated a
salary of £150 *per annum* to him and his successors for ever
and directed that a negro man and woman and four cows
and calves should be purchased for his use and paid for out
of the public treasury. This Act was passed on the 8th
October, 1698.

On the 10th December, in the same year, Mrs. Affra Coming, widow of John Coming, deceased, and a lady of eminent
piety and liberality, made the munificent donation of
seventeen acres of land (then adjoining the town, now in
the very heart of the city) to Mr. Marshall, and his successors, ministers of Charles Town. This is the Glebe land now
held by the two Churches, St. Philip's and St. Michael's;
the same having been divided between them. (*Dalcho's
Church Hist., 32-35.*)

Before learning of the death of Mr. Marshall, the Proprietors had secured the services of the Rev. Edward Marston, M. A., for the settlement on Cooper River, but upon
his arrival in 1700 he was put in charge of St. Philip's
Church in the place of Mr. Marshall, deceased. Unfortunately, Mr. Marston was a person of very different disposition and character from Mr. Marshall. Though
recommended by an Archbishop, as well as by the Bishop
of London, he had been a notorious Jacobite ere his coming
to this Province, and was for a time imprisoned in England
for railing against the government. (*Hist. Am. Epis. Ch.,
Bishop Perry, Vol. 1, 376.*) He brought with him the same
violent passions and contentious disposition. A Jacobite
in England in the reign of William, he turned with equal
rancor against the churchmen in Carolina under Queen
Anne. He espoused the cause of the dissenters against the
establishment of the Church in 1704, and preached most
violently against Sir Nathaniel Johnson, the Governor, and
his party—preparing notes, and keeping them ready for use

in the pulpit if any of that party appeared in the church. The Lay Commission of 1704 was provided especially to get rid of this minister, who refused to forbear from meddling in politics.

During the controversy over the establishment of the Church and the contentions with Mr. Marston, another minister of a name very similar to his came into the Province, and in some way obtained possession of the rectory of St. Philip's and the charge of the church. This was Richard Marsden.

No provision had been made by the government or Church of England for the Episcopal supervision of the clergy who came out to America, and it cannot be denied that many of them were outcasts of the church at home, some of them of the vilest character. Fortunately for the Church in South Carolina, as it happened, blessed with the aid of the Society for the Propagation of the Gospel, in which benefit this Province was the first of all the colonies to participate, her clergymen, after the establishment of the Church, were men of character, full worthy of their high calling. But the scandals of many of the clergymen in the colonies induced the Bishop of London, who claimed a general jurisdiction of all the colonial churches, to send out commissaries, i. e. presbyters charged with the general administration of the Church and supervision of the clergy. The Church having been now established with eight clergymen in this Province, the Bishop of London sent out the Rev. Gideon Johnson, an Irish clergyman who had been recommended by the Archbishop of Dublin to the Bishop of London as a suitable person to act as his commissary in Carolina, requesting that he should be made the minister of Charles Town. After a very tedious passage Mr. Johnson arrived off the bar, and the ship being unable to cross on account of the tide, impatient to get to land he ventured in a small sloop with other passengers to proceed to the town. Unfortunately, a sudden squall coming up, the sloop was driven on a sand bank, supposed to have been Morris Island,

and did not get to the city for some days. Mr. Johnson, whose health was not good, suffered much from the exposure, and his temper, as it appears, still more so. To add to his discomfort, he found Mr. Marsden in the "parsonage house," claiming to be the incumbent of St. Philip's Church. In his distress he poured out bitter complaints to the "Great Bishop" who had sent him out, declaring that he had never repented so much of anything, his sins only excepted, as coming to this place. He described the people to whom he was sent as the vilest race of men on earth, with neither honor, nor honesty, nor religion. Marsden, who was with little doubt an impostor, as he could produce no evidence of ordination, and could give no satisfactory account of the loss of his papers, was finally ousted, and Commissary Johnson duly installed as rector of St. Philip's. Dalcho says that the assiduity and piety of Commissary Johnson soon gained him the affection of the people, and that the laborious duties of his parochial cure so impaired his health that he was given leave of absence for eighteen months, during which time the Rev. Dr. Le Jau, the rector of St. James Goose Creek, officiated once a month at St. Philip's.

In 1711 a free school was established by the General Assembly in connection with the Society for the Propagation of the Gospel, and placed under the care of the Rev. William Guy, A. M., who at the same time was appointed assistant to the rector of St. Philip's. Mr. Guy was the next year removed to the cure of St. Helena, Beaufort, and was succeeded by Thomas Morritt as master of the school, who appears to have been but a deacon at the time, but who having gone to England returned in priest's orders in 1717. A strange thing now happened. Commissary Johnson had been cast away on his coming to the Province upon a sand bank. In the month of April, 1716, the Hon. Charles Craven, Governor of the Province, embarked for England, and Mr. Johnson with thirty other gentlemen went over the bar to take leave of him. Again a sudden squall overset their vessel, and Mr. Johnson, who was in the cabin, lame

with the gout, was unfortunately drowned. It is remarkable
that the vessel is said to have drifted on the same bank on
which Mr. Johnson had nearly perished when he first came
to Carolina, and there his body was found. It was brought
to the town and buried with every mark of respect and sorrow. His parishioners did not know of the character he
had given of them to the Bishop of London, else perhaps
they would not have held Mr. Johnson in such regard.

In England the two systems, the Parish and the Town
or Township, had existed from the most ancient times
side by side, usually but not always coincident in area,
yet separate in character and machinery. The township, which preceded the parish, was the unit of *civil*
and the parish the unit of *ecclesiastical* administration.
(*Blackstone Vol. 1, 112-16. Stubbs Cons. Hist., 1, 227.*)
The Puritans of New England, disaffected to the Church,
adopted the township system to the exclusion of the
parochial. The Churchmen, who settled at Barbadoes,
nearly about the same time, on the other hand established
parishes, and, from time to time adding civil to the ecclesiastical duties of parochial officers, contented themselves
with that organization as the basis alike of civil as of ecclesiastical affairs. The parish thus became the unit alike
of Church and State, and the election precinct of members
of the Commons House of Assembly. The Church Act of
1706 adopted the names of the parishes in Barbadoes for
those in this Province, and in 1712 the care of the poor,
which, under Governor Archdale's act of 1695, had been
committed to overseers, was put under the charge of the
vestries and wardens of the Church in this Province—a
legitimate charge in their ecclesiastical capacity.

In the same year by "*An Act for the better observation of
the Lord's Day, commonly called Sunday*"—which required all
persons to abstain from labor on that day; or from selling
goods; or from travelling, excepting it be to go to a place
of religious worship and to return again, or to visit or relieve
the sick; or from indulging in sports or pastimes—it was
made the duty of the constables, and church wardens of

St. Philip's, once in the forenoon and once in the afternoon, in time of divine service, to walk through the town and to observe, suppress and apprehend all offenders against this law.

In 1716 the Assembly went further and adopted the Parish system of Barbadoes as a model of the government of this colony. From this time until the Revolution, all elections in Charles Town for members of the General Assembly, &c., were held at St. Philip's, the Parish Church, and were conducted by her wardens; and various municipal duties were imposed upon her vestry.

The Fundamental Constitutions had provided that "all towns should be governed by a Mayor, twelve Aldermen and twenty-four of the Common Council," but like most provisions of that most remarkable instrument this was found impracticable. There was but one town in the Province. And though Charles Town had become a place of considerable wealth and importance, it had not yet arrived at a condition to warrant so grand and extensive a government. There was indeed no municipal government before the Revolution. Until that time the law-making power was the same for the town as for the rest of the colony. The General Assembly legislated directly and passed Acts relating to the streets and police regulations and made directly all such municipal ordinances as are usually delegated to a city government. One of the most important and responsible of the duties and powers imposed upon and entrusted to the vestries was that of assessing, levying and collecting the tax for the support of the poor of the parish. This was a peculiarly heavy and troublesome duty of the Vestry of St. Philip's, because of the continual transient poor in the town.

In 1722 an attempt was made to change this system of municipal government, and an Act was passed for the purpose; but an outcry was at once raised against the movement. A petition was addressed to the Hon. James Moore, Speaker, and the rest of the Commons House of Assembly by the major part, it was said, of the inhabitants of Charles

Town against it, and praying for its repeal "as they appre-
hended the consequence thereof will be the desertion of the
town by the inhabitants." Among the signatures to this
protest the number of Huguenot names is very noticeable
as the result of the protest was the retention of so much of
the municipal power in the vestry and wardens of the
Church of England. A memorial was sent to England by
the merchants of Charles Town desiring to be heard by
counsel against the Act, and though Francis Younge, who
was then the agent of the Colonial Government in London,
opposed the memorial, the Lord's Justices in council, upon
a representation of the Board of Trade, approved an order
repealing the Act, and the government of the town was
left as it had been.

The Rev. Alexander Garden arrived in Charles Town in
1719, the year in which the Proprietary government was
overthrown, and was elected Rector of St. Philip's, and
as such he faithfully served the Church for thirty-four
years. (Dalcho's Church History, 98.) In 1710 an Act had
been passed, we have mentioned, "for the erecting of a new
brick church at Charles Town to be the Parish Church of
St. Philip's, Charles Town." Dr. Dalcho states that it is
not known at what period this new church was first opened
for divine service. He supposes that it was probably not
before 1727 when the old church, where St. Michael's now
stands, was taken down. But the exact date has since been
definitely ascertained. Dr. Ramsay, in a note to his
history. (Vol. 2, p. 15.) states that divine service was first
performed in the second St. Philip's Church in 1723, and in
that of St. Michael's in 1761. Bishop Gadsden, in his sermon upon the consecration of the present, the third, St.
Philip's Church building, also mentions that the second St.
Philip's Church, which was burned in 1835, was opened for
worship on Easter Day, 1723. In the report of the committee of the congregation and vestry upon the commemoration of the one hundred and fiftieth year since the congregation of St. Philip's Church had worshipped upon the

present site of the Church, (1874,)* it is said that it was
within the recollection of some then living that there was a
medallion upon the tower of the church bearing the date
"1723"—and such medallion appears upon the engraving of
the building, copies of which have been preserved. There
is a tradition, says the report, that, for some time after the
church was opened, the members of the congregation car-
ried chairs with them upon which they sat during the service. This explains the confusion of the periods fixed for
the opening of the church, 1723 and 1724; the church having
been opened in 1723, before it was completed in 1724 when
the pews were alloted. Dr. Dalcho, writing in 1820, thus
describes the building :

"*St. Philip's* Church stands upon the east side of Church Street, a
few poles north of Queen Street. It is built of brick, and rough cast.
The Nave is 74 feet long ; the vestibule, or more properly, the belfry,
37, the portico 12 feet and 22½ feet wide. The Church is 62 feet wide.
The roof is arched, except over the galleries ; two rows of Tuscan pillars support five arches on each side, and the galleries. The pillars are
ornamented on the inside with fluted Corinthian Pilasters, whose capitals are as high as the cherubim, in relief, over the centre of each arch,
supporting their proper cornice. Over the centre arch on the south
side are some figures in heraldic form representing the infant colony
imploring protection of the King. The Church was nearly finished
when the King purchased the Province of the Lord's Proprietors.
This circumstance probably suggested the idea. Beneath the figures
is this inscription : *Propius res aspice nostras.* This has been
adopted as the motto of the seal of St. Philip's Church. Over the middle arch on the north side is this inscription : *Deus mihi sol*, with ar-
morial bearings, or the representation of some stately edifice.

"Each pillar is now ornamented with a piece of monumental sculp-
ture, some of them with bas-relief figures, finely executed by some of
the first artists in England. These add greatly to the beauty and
solemnity of the edifice. There is no chancel ; the Communion table
stands within the body of the Church. The east end is a panelled
wainscot ornamented with Corinthian pilasters, supporting the cornice
of a fan-light. Between the pilasters are the usual Tables of the Dec-
alogue, the Lord's Prayer and the Apostles Creed. The organ was im-
ported from England, and had been used at the coronation of George

*Note—This commemoration service was held on Sunday, 9th Au-
gust, 1874, the *allotment of pews* having been made in August, 1724;
but the first *service* was held in the Church on Easter Day, 1723.

II. The galleries were added subsequently to the building of the Church. There are 88 pews on the ground floor and 60 in the galleries. Several of the pews were built by individuals at different times with the consent of the vestry. The Communion Plate was a donation to the Church. Two Tankards, one Chalice and Patine, and one large Alms Plate were given by the government and have each the Royal Arms of England engraved on each piece. One Tankard, one Chalice and Patine, and one large Alms Plate have engraved on them : *The Gift of Col. Wm. Rhett, to the Church of St. Philip, Charles Town, South Carolina.* One large Paten, with I. F. R., engraved on it. The pulpit and reading desk stand at the east end of the Church, at the N. E. corner of the middle aisle. The front of the Church is adorned with a portico, composed of four Tuscan columns, supporting a double pediment. The two side doors, which open into the belfry, are ornamented with round columns of the same order, which support angular pediments that project 12 feet; these give to the whole building the form of a cross and add greatly to its beauty. This, however, is somewhat obscured by the intervention of the wall of the grave yard. Pilasters of the same order with the columns are continued round the body of the Church, and a parapet wall extends around the roof. Between each of the pilasters is one lofty sashed window. Over the double pediment was originally a gallery with balusters which has since been removed as a security against fire. From this the steeple rises octagonal ; in the first course are circular sashed windows on the cardinal sides ; and windows with Venetian blinds in each face of the second course, ornamented with Ionic pilasters, whose entablature supports a gallery. Within this course are two bells. An octagonal tower rises from within the gallery, having sashed windows on every other face, and dial plates of the clock on the cardinal sides. Above is a dome upon which stands a quadrangular lantern. A vane, in the form of a cock, terminates the whole. Its height probably is about 80 feet.

"St. Philip's Church has always been greatly admired. Its heavy structure, lofty arches and massive pillars, adorned with elegant sepulchral monuments, cast over the mind a solemnity of feeling highly favorable to religious impressions. The celebrated Edmund Burke, speaking of this Church, says, it 'is spacious and executed in a very handsome taste, exceeding everything of that kind which we have in America;' and the biographer of Whitefield calls it 'a grand Church resembling one of the new churches in London.' "*

The present Meeting Street was originally called Church

*Inscriptions from tablets on the pillars and walls of the Church at the time of its destruction by fire, in 1835, will be found in Dalcho's Church History, pp. 122–126, and in the first Year Book of the City, 1880, (Mayor Courtenay).

Street, but, upon the removal of the congregation of St. Philip's to the present site of the church, the street on which it was erected took the name of Church Street, and the old Church Street became Meeting Street from the white "Meeting House" or Congregational Church, now known as the Circular Church.

The register of births, marriages and deaths still exists from the year 1720, but we have no minutes of the proceedings of the Vestry before 1732. On the 22nd August, 1748, the Vestry ordered "that Mrs. Woolford be again apply'd to about the journal of the Vestry before the year 1732, which, from the demise of Mr. Heyman, the former clerk of the Vestry, hath been missing and acquaint her that unless she will make oath that she hath not that book in her possession or knows not in whose possession it is that she will be prosecuted—that, upon Mrs. Woolford exculpating herself in such manner, an advertisement be put in the Gazette offering a reward of five pounds to any person that shall produce the same." Mrs. Woolford must have exculpated herself, for we find advertisements for the lost minute book in the Gazette of the 6th and 12th of September following. The book was not recovered, and this most valuable historical record is thus lost to us.

By the Church Act of 1706 the vestrymen and wardens were required to take the usual oaths required by Parliament "and likewise to subscribe the test." The minutes for the year 1733 and 1734 contain merely the entry that the vestrymen and wardens took the several oaths and qualified. But at every Easter election afterwards the "test" is written out and subscribed by each vestryman and warden elected. The "test" for 1735, for instance, is in these words:

"We, the Vestry and Churchwardens of the Parish of St. Philip's, Charles-town, who have hereto subscribed our names, do declare that we believe that there is no trans-substantiation whatever in the Sacrament of the Lord's Supper, or in the elements of bread and wine, after consecration thereof by any person whatsoever. Signed the Seventeenth day of April, in the year of Our Lord One Thousand Seven Hundred and Thirty-five."

In the first vestry, of which we have the record, we find the names of three Huguenots—Col. Samuel Prioleau, son of Elias Prioleau the "Pastor" and the most distinguished and prominent of all the Huguenots who came to this Province—Mr. Gabriel Manigault, the son of the emigrant and of Judith Manigault, a most interesting sketch of whose remarkable career is found in the 4th number of the Transactions of the Huguenot Society of South Carolina—and Mr. John Abram Motte, the founder of the distinguished family of that name. These gentlemen, with the other vestrymen, took the oath of "supremacy," subscribed the "test" just quoted, and qualified. We give a few entries from the journals, showing that these offices were no sinecures and indicating the municipal and other duties imposed upon the Vestry and Wardens of the Church, from which it will appear that there is little reason for wonder that persons had to be forced to serve under penalties for refusing.

An account is opened "*The Parish of St. Philip's Church Charles Towne, William Rhett and Henry Housea, Church Wardens.*" It charges them with cash received from Governor Nicholson; from the former church wardens; from "Mr. Joseph Wragg, out of the Sacrament money;" from "a legacy for the poor;" &c. It credits them with "cash gave for the support of John Newton, turned into the streets, £6." "Ditto Thomas Garrat, sick with the flux, £2.10." "Ditto Mary Mathews, in a poor and miserable condition, £15," and so on day by day. We find them collecting fines "for a man swearing without a book;" paying money "for six days working the streets," and "for filling up the pond." In 1742 we find these entries—"10 Nov'm'" "By Ditto received from Benjamin Smith a fine recovered by Justice Gibbs from Peter Brez, for knocking down Mr. Pinckney's negro, £2." "Ditto Mr. Tributed for retailing rum on Sunday, 10s." "Ditto sundry fines received from several persons for walking about streets on Sunday during divine service, 19s. 6d." The same, April 11, 1743, £1. 5s 3d. August 3, 1745. "for a white man beating a negro," £2. "August 7, 1747, by ditto of Mr. Gibbs for persons beating negroes £6. February 24, 1749, received Coll Austin for a white man striking a negro, £2. Ditto James Larden, striking a negro £2," &c., &c.

In 1733 Mr. John Laurens, another Huguenot, father of Henry Laurens, of Revolutionary fame, is elected Church Warden, and on the 9th of April acquaints the Vestry that Dr. John Turner was willing to take care of the poor of the parish and look after them for £100 current money which the Vestry agreed to give. On the 5th July 1734 the Vestry signed the tax list for £1,000 towards the relief and maintenance of the poor—in 1738 the tax list is signed for £1,534 8s. 3d, &c., &c.

In 1734 the Vestry presented a memorial to the Assembly representing the poor accommodation for the lodging and care of the sick and the extravagant charges for the same, the trouble of the officers, and the suffering of the sick in consequence and ask for the appropriation of so much of the square piece of ground belonging to the public in Charles Town as might be necessary whereon to erect proper buildings for the use of the work house and hospital, and for authority to erect buildings at their own proper charge. August 3, 1738, the Wardens advertised that the number of poor and sick suffering from smallpox daily increases, and the cost as well as the difficulty in providing lodging and nurses is so great that they have hired a house and provided proper attention for the reception of all such as are the objects of charity. The hospital was erected (See Statutes Vol. VII–90,) and appears to have been in operation as we find on March 7, 1748, an advertisement in the Gazette that Frederick Holzendorff, chirurgeon, of *St. Philip's Hospital*, in Charles Town, has removed his residence.

The death of Mr. Commissary Johnson in 1716 left the Bishop of London without a representative in this part of his charge. The number of clergymen increasing, the Rev. Alexander Garden was appointed by Dr. Gibson, Bishop of London, in 1726, his commissary for the Provinces of North and South Carolina and the Bahama Islands. We have no record of the conduct of the Rev. Gideon Johnson in the discharge of his duties as Commissary ; but Commissary Garden, we find, held annual visitations regularly in this Province. These visitations were in the form of meetings of the clergy convened for the purpose, at which each clergyman was required to exhibit to the Commissary his Letters of Orders and License to perform the ministerial office in the Province, and a report of his parochial services. A sermon was preached at each of these visitations by some one of the clergy appointed for the purpose. The visitations were held in St. Philip's Church.

From 1742 we find recorded in the journals of the Vestry each year the elections on Monday in Easter week, pursuant to Act of Assembly, not only of the Vestry and Wardens of the Church, but of such municipal officers as five Commissioners of the Highway, five Commissioners of the Market, six Packers, five Wood Measurers and five Fire Masters. Thus were the civil and ecclesiastical affairs of the town settled at the porch of the church.

After the establishment of the Free School by the Assembly, December 12, 1712, the school of the Society for the Propagation of the Gospel was united with the Provincial institution, and the school thus formed was continued in connection with St. Philip's Church until the Revolution. In the year 1728 the Rev. Mr. Morritt was removed from the charge of the school upon his appointment to the cure of Prince George's, Winyaw, and the Rev. John Lambert, A. M., was appointed by the Society their school master in Charles Town and afternoon preacher at St. Philip's Church. He died, however, the following year, and was buried in the church yard, where the stone which marks his grave still stands.* In 1736 the parochial duties of St. Philip's had so increased that the Rector found

---

*See the inscription given in Dalcho's Church History, p. 114.

it impracticable to perform them alone. The Assembly, therefore, May 29. 1736, appropriated £50 sterling *per annum*, to be increased by such further sum as the people might be willing to subscribe, for the support of an assistant, and upon this provision the Vestry, June 8, 1736, solicited the Bishop of London to recommend and appoint some suitable person to assist the Rector in his pastoral duties. The Rev. William Orr, A. M., was accordingly licensed to perform divine service in this Province, and upon his arrival was elected assistant to the Rector.

An attempt was made in 1739 to obtain "a ring of six bells" and a clock for the Church, and the sum of £1,192 currency, equal to £149 sterling, was raised by subscription for the purpose, but the sum was insufficient. Five years later the Vestry ordered a good, plain, substantial church clock, completely fitted for the steeple, to go for eight days, and also a good bell of about 600 weight. They were sent, but upon their arrival proved unsatisfactory. The stroke of the clock was weak, and the bell, the Vestry said, sounded as from a dunghill, and so low that it could not be heard at two or three hundred yards. They were returned.

Two events of interest in connection with St. Philip's Church took place in the year 1740. These were the trial of the Rev. George Whitefield by Commissary Garden's ecclesiastical court, and the great fire of that year.

Mr. Whitefield, who had come out to America to aid Oglethrope in the settlement of Georgia, had previously been to Charlestown. In August, 1738, while about to embark for Europe, he had paid a visit to Commissary Garden, and, at his request, preached in St. Philip's the next Sunday, morning and evening, and was most cordially thanked by him. He returned in 1740, after having had a most wonderful career in England, where his auditories had often consisted of 20,000 persons; but where he had given occasion to the Bishop of London for publishing a charge to his clergy to avoid alike the extreme of enthusiasm and lukewarmness. He had come this time by the way of Philadelphia, and travelling through Pennsylvania, the Jeseys, New York and back again to Maryland, Virginia, North Carolina and this Province, he had preached all along to immense congregations. With Mr. James Habersham's assistance he had founded an orphan asylum in Georgia, which he called Bethesda; and the first collection he made for it was in the Congregational Church in Charlestown—the Circular Church. He had been cordially received in this city (the place, his biographer says, "of his greatest success and the greatest opposition") by Commissary Garden on his first visit; but the enthusiasm, against which the Bishop of London had to warn him, led him here to disregard canonical obligations, which Commisary Garden, charged with the oversight of the clergy in this part of the Bishop of London's jurisdiction, deemed it his duty to enforce. Being often called upon to preach to large crowds, many of whom neither possessed nor knew how to use the Book of Common Prayer in public worship, Whitefield departed from the rule of his Church, making extempore prayers and conducting services without regard to the Prayer Book. This Commissary Garden prohibited, and, Whitefield persisting, he was cited to appear before an ecclesiastical court, held in St. Philip's Church on the 15th July, 1740, to answer for his conduct. He did not himself appear in response to the summons, but Mr. Andrew Rutledge, his counsel, appeared for him and protested against the authority of the Court. The Court overruled the plea to its jurisdiction, and Whitefield appealed to the Lord's Commissioners in England, appointed by the King, for hearing appeals in spiritual causes from his Majesty's plantation in America. The appeal was allowed, but Whitefield did not prosecute it; and after the expiration of the time limited, he having procured no prohibition against the Court's proceeding, it went on with the case, and, Whitefield failing to answer after successive adjournments to allow him an opportunity so to do, judgment of suspension was pronounced against him. (*Dalcho's Church Hist.*, *128–146*.) Unfortunate indeed was it for the Church of England that it could at that time find no means of availing itself of the great work of the Wesleys and of Whitefield; unhappy indeed that it allowed a great and needed revival to end in schism instead of reformation.*

The year 1740 was likewise memorable in the annals of South Carolina, for a destructive fire, which broke out in Charlestown on Tuesday 18th November. It began in a sadler's shop on the south side of Broad Street, between Church Street and East Bay, about 2 o'clock in the afternoon. The houses being generally of wood, and the wind from the northwest, the fire raged with uncontrollable fury, and in four hours consumed every house south of Broad Street besides some on the north side. All the wharves, storehouses, and produce were destroyed. The loss was estimated at nearly one million and a half dollars, and the number of houses destroyed at three hundred. Universal sympathy was exerted for the distresses of the people. A solemn fast was held on Friday, the 28th, and collections were made at the Churches for the benefit of the sufferers. Subscriptions were likewise opened in town and country, and the amount collected, as well as £1,500 appropriated by the General Assembly and £20,000 voted by Parliament, was paid into the hands of the Church Wardens of St. Philip's Church to be distributed according to their discretion among the sufferers. The minute book shows the Vestry and Wardens meeting day after day, receiving contributions and distributing to the poor, and as late as April, 1741, awarding William Osborne £100 currency towards buying a pilot boat, his having been burnt in the time of the fire.

In 1741 the Rev. Mr. Orr, assistant Minister of St. Philip's, was appointed to the mission of St. Paul's Parish; and the Rev. William McGilchrist, who had been sent out by the

*NOTE—The following is represented as the state of the different religious bodies in Carolina in 1740:

Episcopalians.	To the whole as	4½
Presbyterians, French and other Protestants. . . .		4¼ to 10.
Baptists.		1
Quakers.		¼

Society for the Propagation of the Gospel, was appointed in his place at St. Philip's.

We find a curious advertisement, by Mr. Garden, in the South Carolina Gazette of March 11, 1743. It states that the Society for the Propagation of the Gospel, having long at heart the propagation of the Gospel among the negroes and Indian races in his Majesty's colonies in America, had resolved on the following method of pursuing that end, viz : by purchasing some country-born negroes, causing them to be instructed to read the Bible, and in the chief precepts of the Christian religion, and thenceforth employing them as school masters for the same instructions of all negroes and Indian children as might be born in the colonies. The advertisement goes on to state that in pursuance of this plan the Society had purchased, about fifteen months before, two such negroes for this service, and assigned one of them for Charlestown, who would be sufficiently qualified in a few months, and to whom all the negro and Indian children of the parish might be sent for education without any charge to the masters and owners ; and Mr. Garden concludes with an appeal for a voluntary contribution of £400 currency to build a school house for the purpose, which he consents should be put up in a corner of the Glebe land near the parsonage.

This appeal was answered, and in the Gazette of April 2nd, 1744, Dr. Garden publishes an account of receipts and expenditures in which it appears that he had received contributions to the amount of £226. Among the contributors were Hon. Charles Pinckney, Joseph Wragg, Robert Pringle, Jacob Motte, Col. Othniel Beale, Benjamin Smith and Sarah Trott.

The two negro boys so purchased received the baptismal names of Harry and Andrew. The school was established, and the experiment tried in the hope that the negroes would receive instructions from teachers of their own race with more facility and willingness than from white teachers. The school was continued for twenty-two years, first under the supervision of Commissary Garden, as Rector of St.

Philip's, then of his successor, the Rev. Mr. Clarke, and then of the Rev. Robert Smith, afterwards the first Bishop of South Carolina.

The Rev. Commissary wrote to the Society in 1743 that the negro school was likely to succeed and consisted of thirty children. In 1744 upwards of 60 children were instructed in it daily, 18 of whom read in the Testament, 20 in the Psalter, and the rest in the spelling books. In 1746 there were 55 children under tuition, and 15 adults were instructed in the evening. In 1755 there were 70 children in the school, and books were given for their use. In 1757 Mr. Clarke informed the Society that the negro school in Charleston was flourishing and full of children. The Rev. Mr. Smith, during his Rectorship, examined the proficiency of the children twice a week, and the school was deemed in a flourishing condition. But Andrew, one of the teachers, died ; and the other, Harry, "turned out profligate"—and, as the Society had not invested to any greater extent in slaves for educational purposes, they had no other black or colored person to take charge of the school and so it was discontinued.

The Gazette of April 30, 1744, contains this interesting paragraph :

"On Thursday (i. e. 26th April) we had a violent storm of lightning, thunder and rain here. The lightning has done considerable damage to St. Philip's Church, the steeple and organ, and killed Mr. Furniss, who was at work in said church hanging one of the bells. Mr. Isaiah Burnet (Furniss' partner) was knocked down senseless about half an hour, but recovered soon after. One Wilson was also wounded in the knee. The top of the steeple is much shattered, but where the lightning entered on the north side of the church the holes are not above an inch in diameter."

The Gazette of June 11th, 1744, announces another storm, and that the lightning again shattered St. Philip's Church steeple, and struck the organ in the same spot as when Mr. Furniss was killed. It adds that the storm had likewise injured the Dissenters' Meeting House, and that several houses were struck in different parts of the town, yet it did no damage. The injury to the steeple and organ could not have been very great, however, as we can find in the journals no allusion to the incident. The health of the Rev. Mr. McGilchrist failing, he gave notice to the Vestry of his intention to return to England. Whereupon the Vestry applied at once to the Lord Bishop of London to send them out another clergyman to fill his place, and in their letter they make the statement that "the Parish is large, and that the usual auditory in it is six or seven hundred people." Mr. McGilchrist was succeeded on January 25, 1746, by the Rev. Robert Betham, A. M., but he lived a little more than a year after his arrival, dying on the 31st May, 1747, and was succeeded July, 6. 1747, by the Rev. Samuel Quincy; and he having resigned, the Rev. Alexander Keith, Rector of Prince George, Winyaw, succeeded him.

The congregation of St. Philip's outgrew the original Church, and had removed as we have seen to the site of the present edifice in 1723. In less than thirty years it had again outgrown its second edifice. So in 1751 an Act directed "that all that part of Charlestown, situate and lying to the southward of the middle of Broad Street * * * * , be known by the name of the Parish of St. Michael's," and that a church be erected "on or near the place where the old Church of St. Philip's, Charlestown, formerly stood" at a cost to the public of not more than £17,000 proclamation money. The cornerstone was laid February 17. 1752, by his Excellency Governor Glen, which ceremony was followed by a grand dinner. The dinner over, his Majesty's health was drunk, followed by a discharge of the cannon at Granville Bastion; then the health of the Royal Family, and the other Royal toasts. The Gazette adds: The day was concluded with peculiar pleasure and satisfaction. The building of the church did not however progress much faster than had that of St. Philip's. The first Vestry of St. Michael's was not organized until 1759 and the first service was not performed until February, 1761.

The church which still stands is well known for the beauty of its steeple, and is famed for its chime of bells, alike remarkable for their sweetness of tone and romantic history. The cost of the church was £53,535 8s. 9d. currency of the time, about $32,775.87. Of this, £21.877 were subscribed for pews, and £31,656 15s. 9d. were granted by the Assembly.

In the division of the parishes the care of the poor in both were left to St. Philip's, and the Church Wardens and Vestry of St. Philip's were authorized to assess and collect the taxes for the support of the poor as well upon the inhabitants of the Parish of St. Michael's as upon the inhabitants of the Parish of St. Philip's. The representation in the General Assembly was equally divided between the two Parishes; each was to send a Senator, and three Members to the Common House of Assembly. The Rev. Alexander Garden, then Rector of St. Philip's, was allowed £40 proclamation money in lieu of the perquisites he would lose by the division of the Parish. It was provided by the Act that it should be lawful for the inhabitants of either of the two Parishes to bury their dead in the Church yard of the other Parish. The division was at first territorial, and thus it happened that in many families the different branches residing in the different parts of the city were divided. There was a special provision in the Act that no person should own a pew in each Church, unless he owned a house in each Parish. (*Statutes, Vol. VII, 79.*) Besides their distinctive names ("*St. Philip's,*" and "*St. Michael's*") the Churches obtained the appellations of "the Old Church," and "the New Church," and St. Michael's continued to be familiarly called "The New Church" until some time after the burning of "the Old Church" (St. Philip's) in 1835. The writer of this, who is among the last of those baptized in "the Old Church," was accustomed to hear St. Michael's called in his family until the late war "*the New Church.*"

The Rev. Mr. Garden had been Rector of St. Philip's thirty-four years when his increasing infirmities compelled him to seek relief from laborious duties; and he gave notice

to the Vestry that he intended to resign the Rectorship on
or before the 25th March, 1754—Mr. Keith, the assistant
minister, had also given notice of his intention to resign—
the Vestry thereupon wrote to the Bishop of London, requesting him to send out two clergymen in their room. In
their letter to the Bishop the Vestry gave the following
honorable testimony to Mr. Garden's character.

"We should be greatly wanting in duty should we omit to say that
Mr. Garden, during his residence of thirty years and more among us,
has behaved with becoming piety, zeal and candor in his sacred ministry and function, which he hath exercised with unwearied labour and
diligence, to the glory of God and the edification of souls ; and we can
with truth aver he hath been a good Shepherd of Christ's flock."

On Sunday, March 31st, 1754, Mr. Garden preached his
farewell sermon to a crowded audience at St. Philip's
Church from Romans x, 1. Dr. Dalcho gives the conclud-
ing passages of this most touching and eloquent address.

How different is this character which Commissary Garden
gives of the people from that written by his predecessor.
Commissary Johnson, to the Bishop of London :

You know (my Brethren) I abhor flattery; it is sinful at all times,
and would be unpardonable from this sacred place; I am under no
temptation to it; and therefore shall speak forth only the words of
truth and *soberness* concerning the Inhabitants of Charles Town when
I bear this testimony to them, *viz:* that however as in all other com-
munities there are many bad *Individuals* amongst them, too many
despisers of Religion and Virtue, yet, generally speaking, the most
substantial and *knowing* part are a sober, charitable and religiously
disposed people. Nor out of this character do I exclude *Dissenters* of
any denomination with whom I have always lived in all peace and
friendship, and who have always treated me with civility and decent
regard. Would God that there was no *Schism*, no *Dissention* amongst
us; but that all were of *one Mind and one Mouth;* all united in the
same Communion of the Church of *England:* But if this may not be,
to their own Master, they who *dissent*, must stand or fall; let us live in
Peace, friendship and charity towards them. My hope and earnest
desire of my heart and *prayer to God for them* also *is, that they may
be saved.* And moreover I take this opportunity thus publicly to
declare that there is neither *Man, Woman* nor *Child* in the whole
Province of *Carolina* with whom I am not in perfect Charity and to
whom I do not heartily and sincerely wish all happiness, both temporal
and eternal."

We can quote in addition only this last passage :

"Once more, (my beloved Brethren,) *farewell!* May the very God of Peace sanctify you wholly ; and preserve your whole spirits and souls and bodies blameless unto the coming of our Lord Jesus Christ.

"May all the blessings of Heaven descend upon all the inhabitants of this *Province* in general ; those of *Charles Town* in particular ; but more especially on *you*, the beloved people of my late charge—may the ever blessed and glorious Trinity bless you in the *city*, and in the *Field;* in the fruit of your *Body*, the fruit of your *Cattle*, and the fruit of your *Ground*. Bless you in your *Basket ;* and in your *Store*, and in all that you set your Hand unto. Bless you with all the temporal blessings of Health, of Peace and Prosperity ; but above all, and as the Source of all, bless you with truly faithful and obedient Hearts and finally conduct you safe to the Blessed Region of Glory and Immortality."

The Rev. Mr. Garden was beloved, says Dr. Dalcho, by the clergy as a father, and greatly esteemed by the congregation for whose spiritual welfare he had labored so many years. The Vestry, Wardens and Parishioners joined in an address, expressing their reverence and love, and presented to him a piece of plate with an engraving upon it of the west front of the Church and an appropriate inscription. (*See the Address in Dalcho's Church Hist.*, with names thereto, p. 171–174.)

In consequence of the application of the Vestry to the Bishop of London, the Rev. Richard Clarke, A. M., and the Rev. John Andrews, L. L. B., arrived from England in 1753, and were duly chosen Rector and Assistant Minister. Mr. Andrews remained but a short time. He resigned November 9, 1756, and returned to England. Mr. Clarke who was a very learned and able theologian, remained until 1759, when he too returned to England. Mr. Andrews had been succeeded as Assistant Minister by the Rev. Robert Smith, A. M., Fellow of Caius and Gonville College, Cambridge, who now, upon the departure of Mr. Clarke, was chosen Rector, in which position he was to remain for forty-two years. He had for his first Assistant Minister the Rev. Winwood Sergeant, who occupied the position but a very short time, and was succeeded by the Rev. Robert Cooper, (late Rector of Prince William's Parish) December 10, 1759,

who in two years was chosen the first Rector of St.
Michael's. The Rev. Joseph Dacre Wilton arrived from
England at the end of 1761, and was elected assistant January 9, 1762. He died in 1767, and was buried in the
church yard. Mr. Wilton was succeeded by the Rev.
James Crallan, October 14, 1767, who resigned April 25,
1768.

The health of Mr. Smith having suffered from the climate,
he was advised by his physicians to make a voyage to Eng-
land--the Rev. Mr. Cooper and the Rev. Mr. Hart, of
St. Michael's, consenting to supply the Church during his
absence. Mr. Smith remained in England near two years,
and while there engaged the Rev. Robert Purcell, A. M., as
Assistant Minister of St. Philip's. This clergyman had
been curate to the Rector of Shipton-Mallet for eight
years, and was highly recommended for his talents and piety.
He arrived in Charlestown June 18, 1769, and on the 12th
July was elected assistant to the Rector of St. Philip's, a
position which he filled until 1775, when he returned to
England to make some arrangements for the Church at
Shipton-Mallet, where he had left a substitute ; but the war
breaking out he remained in England and received a pen-
sion of £100 *per annum* as a Loyalist.

While in the other colonies most of the clergymen of the
English Church, and most of the Churchmen, were Tories,
the very reverse was the case in South Carolina. The leaders
of the Revolution in this Province were almost all from
old St. Philip's, and with them the Rev. Robert Smith, the
Rector, was in hearty accord. Of the party which Christopher Gadsden assembled under the Liberty Tree, in 1766,
ten of the twenty-six were his fellow worshippers in the
old Church, *to wit*—Wm. Johnson, Joseph Verree, Nathaniel
Lebby, John Hall, Tunis Tebout, William Trusler, Robert
Howard, Alexander Alexander, Edward and Daniel Cannon.
That we are correct in saying that the leaders of the Revolution were most from St. Philip's will be recognized when
we recall well known names of those who led the people

and worshipped in this Church, *to wit*—Christopher Gadsden, Henry Laurens and his son John, Rawlins Lowndes, Col. Charles Pinckney, Charles Cotesworth Pinckney, Thomas Pinckney, the Rutledges (Edward and Hugh—John Rutledge had removed to St. Michael's), Henry Middleton and his son Arthur, William Johnson and Daniel Cannon. Of the sixty principal citizens of South Carolina, upon the fall of Charleston arrested and sent by the British in exile to St. Augustine, in violation of their paroles, more than a third were from St. Philip's, *viz*—Christopher Gadsden, Thomas Ferguson, Peter Timothy, John Edwards, Edward Rutledge, Hugh Rutledge, Isaac Holmes, William Hasell Gibbes, Alexander Moultrie, John Earnest Poyas, Doctor Peter Fayssoux, Edward McCrady, John Neufville, William Johnson, Thomas Grimball, Anthony Toomer, Robert Cochran, Thomas Hall, Arthur Middleton, Samuel Prioleau, Jr., Edward Weyman, Henry Crouch, and John Splatt Crips. And so it was that, when in the outset of the Revolution the Provincial Congress set apart the 17th February, 1778, as a day of fasting, humiliation and prayer, the Commons House of Assembly, with the silver Mace (the same which still lies upon the Speaker's desk during a session of our present House of Representatives) borne before them, went in procession to St. Philip's Church, where a pious and excellent sermon was preached before them by the Rector, the Rev. Robert Smith, for which he received the thanks of the body. Mr. Smith continued to officiate during the Revolution until Charlestown fell into the hands of the British, when he was banished to Philadelphia and his property confiscated. The Rev. Charles Frederick Moreau took charge of the Church during the British occupancy of the city.

The Rev. Robert Smith, upon his return from exile after the Revolution, in May, 1783, was joyfully welcomed by the inhabitants of Charlestown generally. St. Philip's in particular gladly hailed the arrival of their honored and beloved minister. The deranged state of the finances of the Church at this period, as well as of his own estate which

had been sequestered by the British, made it necessary
for him to add to the great and multiplied labors
of his pastoral function the arduous and anxious
responsibility of tuition. He organized an academy,
for which he spared neither trouble nor expense in ob-
taining the best qualified classical teachers, and which
afterward, upon the passage of an Act establishing the
Charleston College in 1785, became incorporated with
that institution, of which he was appointed the principal. It was also, says Dalcho, through his unwearied exertions that the Vestries of St. Philip's and St. Michael's
were led to associate in a convention for the purpose of
sending delegates to a General Convention of the Episcopal Church in the United States. This was the beginning
of the Diocesan Convention, or Council as it is now called,
in South Carolina. He attended the General Convention
held in 1786 at Wilmington, Delaware. In 1789 Mr.
Smith received the degree of Doctor of Divinity from
the University of Pennsylvania. In 1795 he was elected
the first Bishop of the Protestant Episcopal Church in
South Carolina, and was consecrated at Christ Church,
Philadelphia, on the 13th September of that year. Bishop
Smith established the precedent of remaining pastor, notwithstanding his elevation to the episcopate, which was
followed by his three successors in office. In 1786 the Rev.
Thomas Frost arrived from England, whence he had come
at the invitation of Dr. Smith as his assistant, and remained
in that station until the death of Bishop Smith in 1801
when he became Rector, but unhappily survived only until
1804.

The Revolution had left the Church in an anomalous
condition. Under the law of England the "parson" or
Rector was a corporation sole, in whom the property of the
Church was vested. But the Church had been disestablished
by the Constitution of 1778; and the title to the property
formerly vested in the parson was a matter of legal ques-
tion. [It does not appear that any division of the Glebe

lands given by Mrs. Affra Coming had been made between St. Philip's and St. Michael's Churches upon the creation of St. Michael's Parish, but the interest of St. Michael's in them was recognized.] To meet this condition of affairs, in 1785 an Act was passed incorporating the Vestries and Church Wardens of the two Parishes into one corporate body, with power to hold and dispose of the lands and other property then vested in the said Churches or any other they might acquire. (*Statutes 8, Vol. 168.*) This arrangement did not, however, work well, and so in 1791 the Vestries and Wardens of the two Churches obtained from the Legislature another Act making the two Churches separate and distinct bodies politic and corporate. (*Ibid. 168.*) Before the passage of this Act an agreement had been entered into by the two Churches for a division of the Glebe lands. This agreement was confirmed by the Act separating the Churches. It was not, however, until the year 1797 that a formal deed of partition was executed by the two bodies. In this division St. Philip's Church obtained the greater quantity of land, most of which, however, was at the time vacant and unimproved; while St. Michael's obtained most of the improved property with a more regular income.

By the State Constitution of 1790 Charleston, including the two Parishes of St. Philip's and St. Michael's, was made one election precinct, with fifteen members of the House of Representatives— and two Senators, one for each of the Parishes. This was the origin of the allowance of two Senators to the City of Charleston, which continued until the Constitution of 1895. The Senators and Representatives were styled *from the Parishes of St. Philip's and St. Michael's*, not *from Charleston.*

When Mr. Frost became Rector in 1801, the Rev. Peter Manigault Parker, the first native born South Carolinian to enter the ministry of the Church, became Assistant Minister, but lived only about a year after. Upon the death of Mr. Frost the Rev. George Pogson, Rector of St. James Goose Creek, officiated during that summer; and then the Rev. Edward Jenkins, Rector of St. Michael's, was called, and accepted the charge of St. Philip's December 2, 1804, and the Rev. William Percy was elected a temporary or third Minister of St. Philip's and St. Michael's conjointly In the Spring of 1807 Dr. Jenkins went to England, leaving the Rev. James Dewar Simons to officiate during his absence. Dr. Jenkins resigned the next year, and Mr. Simons was elected Rector August 7, 1809. The Rev. Christopher Edwards Gadsden, Minister of St. John's Berkeley, was elected assistant December 21, 1809, when Dr. Percy ceased to officiate at St. Philip's. The Rev. Mr. Simons died May 27, 1814, and Mr. Gadsden became Rector. The Rev. Thomas D. Frost, son of the Rector, became Assistant Minister March 12, 1815, and died May 16, 1819. The Rev. Alston Gibbs officiated the remainder of the year.

St. Philip's Church had escaped the great fires which had devastated the city in 1740, 1778, 1796, and in 1810. In that of 1796 the French Protestant Church, but a short distance from it, was burned, and the steeple of St. Philip's was on fire but was saved by the gallant conduct of a negro man who climbed to the burning shingles and tore them off, for which service he obtained his freedom. It had only escaped these great conflagrations to be destroyed at last in one of much smaller extent, on Sunday morning, February 14, 1835. We take the following account of its destruction from The Courier, of February 16, 1835 :

* * * "The most striking feature of this calamity is the destruc tion of St. Philip's Church, commonly known as the Old Church. The venerable structure, which has for more than a century (having been built in 1723) towered among us in all the solemnity and noble proportions of antique architecture, constituting a hallowed link between the past and the present, with its monumental memorials of the beloved and honored dead, and its splendid new organ (which cost $4,500), is now a smoking ruin. Although widely separated from the burning houses by the burial ground, the upper part of the steeple, the only portion of it externally composed of wood, took fire from the sparks which fell upon it in great quantities. It is much to be regretted that preventive measures had not been taken in season to save the noble and consecrated edifice. The flames slowly descending wreathed the steeple, constituting a magnificent spectacle and forming literally a pillar of fire, and finally enwrapped the whole body of the church in its

enlarged volume. The burning of the body of the church was the closing scene of the catastrophe. In 1796 it was preserved by a negro man who ascended it and was rewarded with his freedom for his perilous exertions, and again in 1810 it narrowly escaped the destructive fire of that year, which commenced in the house adjoining the Church yard on the north.

"We have been informed that the only monument of the interior of the church which was not totally destroyed is one that with an accidental appropriateness bears the figure of grief."

The Rev. John Johnson, D. D., the present Rector of St. Philip's Church, in his sermon preached on Sunday, August 9, 1874, in commemoration of the one hundred and fiftieth year of the occupation of the present site of the church for divine service, speaking of the Rectorship of the "dear old Dr. Gadsden," says:

" It is his ministry also which really bridges over a great chasm in the history of the Parish. I mean the destruction of the Old Church by fire, and the worshipping by the congregation in a temporary frame building erected in the middle of the western church yard. Dr. Gadsden had been your Rector for twenty-one years, when on that fatal Sunday morning in February, of the year 1835, the flakes of the fire from the north of us caught the dry wood work of our steeple, and the flames descending wrapt the Church of so many consecrated affections, until despite all efforts ' our holy and once beautiful house where our fathers praised God, was burned up with fire, and all our pleasant things laid waste.'

" It is not too much to say that never before or since in the history of this city has the loss of a public building been attended with more poignant sorrow and mourning than that of old St. Philip's Church. To show how general the feeling in our community, our congregation had places of worship offered them by many of their fellow Christians of all denominations. And one occurrence during the fire was made the subject of some lines by, it is thought, Mr. Charles Fraser, once an honored citizen but not of our flock.

" I can remember only the spectacle of the burning at a distance, and the sounds of grief that were close by me as I watched the flames, but knew not how to estimate in my childhood *such* a loss.

" Men talked of speedily replacing it, but it could never be done; in its most sacred associations and its time hallowed adornments we knew there could be but one 'Old St. Philip's.' Such losses laugh to scorn insurance money. Such ruins when they fall shake the very ground of our lives, and strew with ashes our bruised and desolated hearts. How while the ruins were still smoking on that Sunday morning the affected flock were gathered by their Shepherd as well as they could be, in the old Sunday School building to the east of us, and how to a weeping congregation, he preached Christ's own message of comfort and consolation," &c.

It was really with remarkable energy and liberality that the present church was built. For those times were, like the present, in a most depressed condition. In answer to objections to public aid in the rebuilding of the church, because it was said the congregation was a rich corporation, the Vestry state, in the Southern Patriot, of the 19th February, 1835, that in the last few years some of the building leases of the Glebe lands having expired the Vestry were obliged to pay for the improvements upon them, when, from the depreciation of property, the land and buildings could scarcely be sold (in some cases) for the sums which they had to pay for the buildings alone. This, it will be remembered, was just before the great financial panic of 1837. Notwithstanding this, Dr. Johnson points out that on the 12th of November of that year the corner-stone of the new building was laid with appropriate ceremonies; the first service under its roof was held on a fast day, the 3rd May, 1838; and the church was consecrated by Bishop Bowen on the 9th day of November, 1838.

The author is indebted to the Rev. Dr. Johnson for the following interesting account of the rebuilding of the church :

"Soon after the destruction of the second church by fire, on the 14th February, 1835, the present edifice was planned and its corner-stone was laid 12th November, 1835. The architect was Mr. J. Hyde. Built of brick on the same foundations, except with extension of twenty-two or twenty-three feet to the eastward, or chancel end, the ground plan of the new church was nearly the same as that of the old one. The differences were as follows : The floor was raised above ground about three feet ; steps of stone being used to ascend to the three porches at the west end of the building, and to the two door-ways central on the side walls; a chancel, recessed about fifteen feet, and lighted with a wide and lofty window, proved an important addition to the interior; the two side-aisles were put immediately next to the side walls; one hundred and two pews on the floor provided five hundred and fifty sittings, while sixty-six in the galleries, reached by stairs in the vestibule, provided two hundred and fifty more, making accommodations, without crowding, for upwards of eight hundred persons. But, with seats arranged along the aisles and in the vestibule, as has been done for special occasions, the capacity of the church may be assumed as about twelve hundred sittings. So, in regard to its external appearance, the *new* differs not greatly from the *old* building. The three characteristic porches, north, south and west, were repeated, each with four columns supporting entablature and pediment. As before, a stately square tower, rising above these porches into a steeple of octagonal section, dominates the building. But, continued upwards, as the former was not, into a spire two hundred feet high, after the design of Edward B. White, architect, the steeple is surmounted by a plain gilded cross.

"So great was the love of the congregation for their old church-building, that they entertained for a while no other thought than to reproduce, as far as possible, the edifice they had lost. But within a year, other counsels prevailed; and the new plans, as has been seen, departed in some important particulars from the old. Both structures retained the interior features of the Georgian period of London church architecture, viz., galleries for congregation and choir, the latter over the entrance to the middle aisle, and a high pulpit adapted to the galleries.

"The same orders of architecture also were retained within and without, but with modifications that were improvements. Thus, the massive, square piers that supported the old church, that gave it some grandeur, and, faced with fluted pilasters bearing fine sculptured memorial tablets, some grace also, were not repeated because they darkened the interior, and interfered seriously with vision and hearing. The Doric order of the later (Roman) period gave rule, measure, and proportion to the exterior of the new church, so that the columns, pilasters and entablatures without the building represent very correctly, in all but the ornaments* of capital and frieze, the order they illustrate. The interior of the sacred edifice is finished in the Corinthian order of architecture, and is the only specimen in the city of that order, with all the rich ornaments of the later, or Roman, period.† These are executed, for the most part, in stucco, but the capitals of the columns are of carved wood. The roof and galleries are supported by eight fluted columns, four on each side, rising from pedestals of the same level as the rail of the pews to the height of twenty feet above the floor. There, these columns, finished with their appropriate capitals, meet the line of the entablature, not extended in the usual way from column to column, but circumscribed above each column, so as to produce, with the overhanging cornice, the effect of a higher and larger capital, which, of course, it is not. This departure from conventional design is something almost in the way of a *"jeu d' esprit."* But it has its reason in the precedent of one of the finest London churches, designed by James Gibbs, architect, 1721, and the express wish of the Charleston congregation to secure, thereby, the light and airy effect of the English prototype.

"At a meeting of the congregation of St. Philip's, 27th June, 1836, it was Resolved, "That the heavy pillars of the interior of the church be dispensed with, and that in lieu thereof, Corinthian columns (as far as practicable) after the style of St. Martin's in the Fields, London, be adopted." And again, Resolved, "That the pillars of the plans presented be lowered, so as to reduce the arches." These arches were the motive of the whole scheme. Springing longitudinally from the square of cornice above each col-

*These appear in the columns, and on the frieze, of the Market Hall, Charleston.

†The earliest (Grecian) Corinthian column is seen in the colonnade of the Charleston Hotel.

umn, at an altitude of about twenty-five feet, and rising at
their crown to a level of thirty-six feet above the floor,
these fine arches on each side support the roof, and contri-
bute no little to the beauty of the interior, lifting the eye
above the columns and galleries to the topmost height of
the main arched ceiling of the church, forty-two or three feet
above the floor. The crown of each arch is ornamented
with a cherub's head and wings in stucco, while, in the space
of the spandrels, between the shoulders of the arches,
the same material is used for the display of the acanthus
ornamentation. The unbroken entablature is seen in the
chancel where it passes from one pilaster to another, but is
again broken by the head of the high, stained-glass window.
Above the cornice of the chancel, the coved ceiling is
ribbed and paneled with rosettes in stucco. On either side
of the chancel, the walls are enriched by tablets, inscribed
with "the Creed, the Lord's Prayer, and the Ten Command-
ments." The Holy Table, saved from the old church while
it was burning down, still continues to be used in the services, an emblem of union and communion between the
generations of St. Philip's, past, present and future. A ves-
try-room has been built in recent years in the northeastern
angle of the church.

DIMENSIONS OF THE EXTERIOR.

Extreme length of building, not including the western porch. .120 feet
Extreme width of building, not including the south and north
    porches .... 62 "
Projection of porches...................................... 12 "
Height of walls on sides .... 35 "
Height of ridge of roof .... 45 "
Height of steeple ....200 "

DIMENSIONS OF THE INTERIOR.

Extreme length of church ....114 feet
Depth of chancel .... 9 "
Width of chancel .... 24 "
Extreme width of church ....:................... 56 "
Height of galleries (upper rail) .... 14 "
Extreme height of ceiling................................... 42 "
Width of vestibule .... 20 "

"The cost of the new church, as reported to the congregation, 15th July, 1839, was $84,206.01. The subsequent expense of erecting a steeple must have raised the total cost to nearly $100,000."*

At the time of the burning of the Old Church the ardent, gifted and lamented Daniel Cobia was Assistant Minister. His ministry was brief; of but three years; it was almost entirely spent in the temporary building called the Tabernacle. His eloquent voice was not heard in the present edifice—he died in 1837, and was succeeded by the Rev. Abraham Kaufman, whose ministry was equally brief, whom all had begun to admire, and sorrowed thus to lose. Tablets to their memories lie at the foot of the chancel in the present church. The Rev. John Barnwell Campbell succeeded Mr. Kaufman as Assistant Minister in 1740, serving for twelve years in that station.

Upon the death of Mr. Calhoun the City Council of Charleston unanimously passed a resolution that, in their opinion, the City of Charleston, the chief metropolis of the State, might with propriety ask for herself the distinction of being selected as the final resting place of that illustrious man, and that the Mayor, in behalf of the Council and the citizens of Charleston, should communicate with the family of the deceased and earnestly entreat that the remains of him they loved so well should be permitted to repose among them. This request was acceded to; the body was brought to this city and received with the grandest, the most imposing and solemn ceremonies. St. Philip's Church yard was at once designated as the temporary resting place. There were two reasons for this selection. First, the close historic connection of the church with the commonwealth of which Calhoun was the greatest product; and, secondly, there was a peculiar fitness in the circumstance that Bishop Gadsden, the Rector of St. Philip's, had been a class-mate

---

*On the inside walls of the present church are monumental tablets to Bishop Christopher E. Gadsden, the Rev. William Dehon, William Mason Smith, and Mrs. Mary Ann Elizabeth Cogdell—and in the vestibule is one to Maj. Gen. William Moultrie, erected by the Society of the Cincinnati.

of the great man at Yale College. And so we read in the account of that grand funeral pageant:

"The next day, the 26th April, i. e. the day after the reception of the body and its lying in state in the City Hall, was appointed for the removal of the remains to the tomb. At early dawn the bells resumed their toll; business remained suspended, and all the evidences of public mourning were continued.

"At 10 o'clock a civic procession, under the direction of the Marshal, having been formed, the body was then removed from the catafalque in the City Hall and borne on a bier by the guards of honor to St. Philip's Church; on reaching the Church, which was draped in the deepest mourning, the cortege proceeded up the central aisle to a stand covered with black velvet, upon which the bier was deposited. After an anthem sung by a full choir, the Right Reverend Dr. Gadsden, Bishop of the Diocese, with great feeling and solemnity, read the burial service, to which succeeded an eloquent funeral discourse by the Rev. Mr. Miles.* The holy rites ended, the body was again borne by the guard of honor to the western cemetery of the Church to the tomb erected for its temporary abode, a solid structure of masonry raised above the surface and lined with cedar wood. Near by, pendant from the tall spar that supported it, drooped the flag of the Union, its folds mournfully sweeping the verge of the tomb as swayed by the passing wind, enwrapped in the pall that first covered it on reaching the shores of Carolina. The iron coffin, with its sacred trust, was lowered to its resting place, and the massive slab, simply inscribed with the name 'Calhoun,' adjusted to its position."

It was ultimately decided that there was no fitter place in the State for the repose of Mr. Calhoun's remains than where they had been laid; and that there they should remain. It being feared during the late war that, if the city should fall into the enemy's hands, despite might be done to the remains of him who was regarded as the great apostle of Southern rights, and whose doctrines, it was said, had brought on the war, his tomb was quietly and secretly opened, and the coffin containing them removed to another place in the eastern church yard where they remained until the war was over, when they were as quietly restored to the original tomb.

In December, 1883, Mr. Charles Inglesby, a member of St. Philip's Church, then a Representative in the State Legislature from Charleston, introduced a Joint Resolution

*Rev. James W. Miles.

appropriating funds for the construction and erection of a Sarcophagus upon the grave. The Resolution recited that:

"Whereas, upon the announcement in March, 1850, of the lamented death of the late Senator John C. Calhoun, the State of South Carolina claimed the privilege of taking into its custody his remains, and did cause them to be removed, with the highest public honors, to the City of Charleston for burial ;

"And whereas, for want of time it was only then possible to erect a temporary structure in which Senator Calhoun's remains could be deposited ;

"And whereas, by reason of the many public disabilities since accruing, which have prevented the intended action of the General Assembly in the construction of an appropriate sarcophagus of enduring material, suitably inscribed, in which the remains of South Carolina's distinguished son may be forever preserved ;

And whereas, the time is now opportune for discharging this high public duty."

With this recital the Joint Resolution was passed unanimously, appropriating the sum of three thousand dollars for the "erecting in St. Philip's Church yard, in the City of Charleston, of a sarcophagus for the remains of John C. Calhoun, which are there buried." (*18th Stat. of S. C., 661.*) With the sum so appropriated the sarcophagus was erected.* Dr. Johnson kindly furnishes this description of the tomb:

THE SARCOPHAGUS OF CALHOUN.

"Situated in the centre of the western cemetery of St. Philip's Church, and in direct extension of the line of its length from east to west, this sarcophagus holds the mortal remains of South Carolina's great statesman. It is built of polished granite, rising from a base of 10 by 6 feet to a total

---

* "The massive slab, simply inscribed with the name 'Calhoun'"—which (so grand in its simplicity) marked the temporary tomb and had to be moved to make way for the State's Sarcophagus—is fixed in vertical position against the south wall of St. Philip's Sunday School Building, in the northeast corner of the eastern cemetery, and bears the following additional inscription:

" *This marble for thirty-four years covered the tomb of CALHOUN in the Western Churchyard. It has been placed here by the Vestry, near the spot where his remains were interred during the siege of Charleston, from which spot they were afterwards removed to the original tomb, and subsequently deposited under the Sarcophagus erected on the same site in 1884 by the State.*"

height of 10 feet. The iron coffin rests between the spaces prepared for it in the base just mentioned, and in a heavy block, 4 by 8 feet, superimposed upon it. Four highly polished columns, one at each angle of the superstructure, support a solid mass of entablature and pediment, covering and finishing the structure in rectangular dimensions, somewhat less than those of the base first described. The inscriptions are as follows:

[North Side.]

ERECTED BY THE STATE OF SOUTH CAROLINA.

[South Side.]

JOHN CALDWELL CALHOUN.

BORN MARCH 18, 1782.

DIED MARCH 31, 1850.

[East Side.]

REPRESENTATIVE IN THE LEGISLATURE.

MEMBER OF CONGRESS.

UNITED STATES SENATOR.

[West Side.]

SECRETARY OF WAR.

VICE-PRESIDENT.

SECRETARY OF STATE.

A beautiful and vigorous Magnolia tree, planted near the sarcophagus, on the western side, rises some thirty feet above it; and, perennially green, typifies the undying reputation of the man, as well as the unchanging affection of the people who were most dear to him."

Upon the death of Bishop Gadsden, in 1852, the Rev. John Barnwell Campbell became Rector; and the Rev. Christopher P. Gadsden, the deceased Bishop's nephew, became Assistant Minister, remaining as such for six years, when he became Rector of St. Luke's. Mr. Campbell resigned in 1858, and in 1859 the Rev. William R. Dehon became Rector, and the Rev. W. B. W. Howe Assistant Minister. Mr.

Dehon died in 1862, and Mr. Howe succeeded him as Rector in 1863.

When the steeple of St. Philip's Church was completed, early in the decade of the fifties, a clock, with a chime of bells attached so as to ring tunes by the clock work, was presented to the church by Mr. Colin Campbell, of Beaufort, S. C., an uncle of the then incumbent Rector, the Rev. John Barnwell Campbell. The bells were taken down in the beginning of the war and given to the Confederate Government to be cast into cannon.

During the late war the steeples of St. Philip's and St. Michael's, the most conspicuous objects in the city from a distance, served as targets for the great guns with which the city was bombarded. St. Philip's suffered particularly. Ten or more shells entered its walls. The chancel was destroyed, the roof pierced in several places, and the organ demolished.

The congregation had continued to worship in the church, after the bombardment had begun, until the 19th November, 1863, that day being a Thanksgiving Day, when, during the delivery of the sermon by the Rector, a shell fell and burst near the church. It was during this time that the Rector, the Rev. W. B. W. Howe, so endeared himself to the congregation and community at large. The Rev. Dr. Johnson, the present Rector of the church—himself the Engineer Officer of Fort Sumter, by whose skill, patient labor and bravery the crumbling walls of the fort were rendered tenable—thus speaks of Mr. Howe's conduct at this time:

" Upon the background of the political troubles, the exciting times, the agitated feelings of that period, Mr. Howe ministered with a calm unswerving fidelity, a gentle tact, a good judgment, a firm hold on the people's affections. While some flocks scattered, and some shepherds left the threatened and beleaguered city to minister to the refugees in the interior of the State, the Rector of St. Philip's hesitated not to stay here from the beginning to the ending of the war in active discharge of the duties of his station. Though the congregation continued to be large, he found time to visit assiduously the sick and wounded in the hospitals. Though the sound of battle grew nearer from Port Royal to James Island in 1861 and 1862, and the smoke of battle hung around our harbor in the spring and summer of 1863, the regular services of the church were maintained in this building. And it was not until the autumn of 1863, that, while the Rector was preaching one Sunday in his pulpit, a shell fired upon the city from the enemy's batteries on Morris Island, was heard to fall and explode in the western church yard. The congregation sat until the sermon was concluded in the regular time and manner. But from that date the religious services at St. Philip's were discontinued, the doors were shut, the damages of the bombardment proceeded, and the building came in for its share of them."

Bursting shells drove also the congregations of St. Michael's and Grace away from their churches, and they, with the congregation of St. Philip's, united for worship, on Advent Sunday, 1863, in the spacious Church of St. Paul's. Here the Rev. Mr. Howe, in connection with the Rev. Mr. Keith and the Rev. Mr. Elliott, Minister and Assistant Minister of St. Michael's, ministered the consolations of the Gospel to a large flock until the first Sunday in Lent, March 5, 1865.

Mr. Howe, then alone remaining in charge of the mixed congregation, upon the fall of the city was required by the Federal military authorities to pray for the President of the United States. This his allegiance to the Confederate Government forbid as long as the war continued; and, like one of his predecessors in the Rectorship of St. Philip's and also in the Bishopric of the Diocese, he was banished from the city. Bishop *Smith* was banished from the city for refusing to use the prayer for the *King of England;* Bishop *Howe* was banished for refusing to use the prayer for the *President of the United States.*

Upon the return of the members of the congregation, at the end of the war, steps were at once taken to repair the church, so far at least as to allow services to be resumed. The Vestry, which had been elected at Easter, 1864, held over, and at once took steps to this end. Mr. James T. Welsman, a member of the congregation, most generously advanced the money necessary; and divine service was resumed in the church, after an interval of two years and nearly

four months, on Sunday, the 4th March, 1866, with a large
congregation then and there assembled. Upon this occasion
Rev. Mr. Howe, the Rector, preached a most eloquent sermon from the text: "I am the Lord, I change not; therefore ye sons of Jacob are not consumed," Malachi iii, 6, in
which he thus touchingly and manfully referred to the
events which had occurred since the congregation had separated, after the service on that memorable Thanksgiving
Day, in 1863, when the enemy's shells were falling around
them :

"Beloved brethren, we who are here present before God have all of
us met of late some of the great problems of life, not in the schools of
the philosophers, or in the verses of the poet, or in the pages of the
historian, or in the experiences of others, but in our own persons, and
that, too, eye to eye, and face to face. Is it not a cause for congratula-
tion, then, that not our faith, nor our love, nor our knowledge, which
may fail in the 'hour and power of darkness' is to be our stay and support, but our Heavenly Father, who is greater than all, and who will
not permit 'tribulation or distress, or persecution or famine, or naked-
ness or peril, or sword,' to pluck us out of our great Redeemer's hands?
Yes, it is the unchangeable faithfulness of our God toward His people—
unchangeable in all the vicissitudes of life, and faithful where all else
is false—which can alone in seasons of great trial enable us to come off
conquerors; and it is to this faithfulness, therefore, that I would now
especially point you. I wish, before I conclude, to contemplate my
text in relation to our immediate present and to the past four years.
My own absence from you for a twelve month, and the re-assembling of
the congregation for the first time after the lapse of more than two
years within these hallowed and dear walls, so sadly eloquent of days
that are past, must be my excuse, if any is needed, for handling at this
time and place our grievous wounds, and which, if I uncover for a mo-
ment, God knows it is NOT to 'put a tongue in them that should move the
stones of Rome to mutiny,' but to heal them, if they may be healed.
At all events, I will pour upon them the only wine and oil that in my
heart I believe *can* heal them.

"Shall I then seek to persuade you of a brilliant future, and in it
ask you to forget the past? Shall I ask you to transfer your affections
from the Union of our Fathers to one which asserts a French Republi-
canism? Brethren, I will be guilty of no such quackery as this. I pray
that a prosperous future may be in store for us, if God wills, and will
labor together with you to bring it to pass; but even the prospects of
such a future cannot heal those who in the late war contended for principles more than for results. How then, as Christian men, shall we
view *present results?* Shall we view them as condemning the cause

for which we prayed and suffered and died, and as proclaiming it to be an unrighteous cause ? For one I am this day as satisfied of its justness, consonance with previous American principles, as when I last spoke to you from this pulpit, and you listened in your present places while shells from distant cannon burst around us. It is due to the living, who entered upon that contest sincerely, and who still feel that its merits are unaffected by results, to say thus much ; and it is due also to our gallant dead, who did not count their lives dear unto themselves, to say it. History indeed will do them justice as she weighs in impartial balance the cause for which they fell ; but it ill becomes us to put a seal upon our lips and delegate to the future their vindication ; but now, this day, and all the days of our lives, to say of them what Pericles said from the bema, outside the walls of Athens, over those Athenians who fell in the first year of the Peloponnesian war : ' Therefore, in behalf of such a city as Athens is, these men, whose bones we have laid in yonder mound, died fighting bravely, rightly judging that she ought not to be robbed of all that made her glorious. Let us who survive, like them, be willing to suffer for her sake.' Not a whit behind these countrymen of Pericles were our fathers and husbands and brothers and sons who now sleep upon many a battlefield in these once fair, but now desolated Southern States, and who, like the children of Athens more than two thousand years ago, fell fighting bravely in behalf of the traditions of their fathers, of Southern civilization, and of the rights of self-government. That they fell in behalf of the weaker side cannot tarnish their fair fame. Rather do we who survive feel that in their graves lie buried beyond a resurrection the fruits of ancestral toil, and all that once made us proud of the name of American," &c., &c.

The church-building had been repaired only sufficiently to allow the services to be resumed, and in 1877 it became necessary to have a complete and thorough reparation and restoration of the edifice. This was undertaken and accomplished at large expense. But by economy and careful management so successfully were the affairs of the church conducted, that not only had all the expense of restoration been met and discharged, but the congregation had, at a cost of $11,000.00, purchased a building adjoining the eastern church yard, on the south, which had been an hotel, and converted it into a Church Home for indigent ladies of the congregation—when another terrible calamity befell. The Vestry of the Church had had a meeting on the afternoon of the 31st August, 1886, at which time the reports of the committees showed that all debts incurred by the restoration from its injuries in the war, and upon all other accounts, excepting one still remaining from the original building of the church, which was amply secured, had been fully paid and discharged, when in a few hours the church was again in ruins from the appalling earthquake of that night. The walls were cracked, the west porch destroyed, the north and south porches shattered, the roof was broken through by the fall of iron columns and bricks from the steeple, the galleries dislocated, the chancel walls were cracked. The steeple was very much injured, the iron column and brick arches in the lantern were thrown down. The cost of repairing the building from this second disaster was little less than $20,000.

The following named clergymen have gone forth from St. Philip's Church, most of whom were baptized at her font: The Reverends Peter Manigault Parker, James Dewar Simons, Christopher Edwards Gadsden (Bishop), Alston Gibbs, Paul Trapier Gervais, Edward Rutledge, Thomas D. Frost, Edward Neufville, Maurice Harvey Lance, Francis H. Rutledge (Bishop), Philip Gadsden, Alexander Marshall, Edward Phillips, Daniel Cobia, Charles Cotesworth Pinckney, Jr., James Maxwell Pringle, Christopher P. Gadsden, Roberts Poinsett Johnson, P. F. Stevens, James W. Miles, Edward R. Miles, Lucien C. Lance, Henry L. Phillips, Thomas F. Gadsden, J. Mercier Green, John Johnson, F. Marion Hall, William H. Moreland, Edward McCrady,* and J. W. Cantey Johnson.

The following is a list of the Clergy of the Church for two hundred and seventeen years. During all of this time it will be observed that there have been but sixteen Rectors, and what is more remarkable that the joint terms of four of these cover a period of one hundred and thirty-five years, to wit: Commissary Garden, 35 years; Bishop Smith, 42 years; Bishop Gadsden, 32 years; and the present Rector, Dr. Johnson, 26 years. There have been during that time twenty-four Assistant Ministers.

---

*The son of Prof. John McCrady.

Rectors.

Atkin Williamson......................1680–....
Samuel Marshall.....................1696–1699
Edward Marston.....................1699–1705
Richard Marsden 1705–1707
Gideon Johnson (Commissary) 1707–1716
Alexander Garden (Commissary) 1719–1754
Richard Clarke 1755–1759
Robert Smith (First Bishop of So. Ca.).........1759–1801
Thomas Frost 1801–1804
Edward Jenkins 1804–1809
James Dewar Simons.....................1809–1814
Christopher E. Gadsden (Bishop) 1814–1852
John Barnwell Campbell................. 1852–1858
William Dehon 1859–1862
William B. W. Howe (Bishop) 1863–1872
John Johnson (the present incumbent) 1872

Assistant Ministers.

Thomas Morritt 1717–1728
John Lambert 1728–1729
William Orr...........................1737–1741
William McGilchrist......................1741–1745
Robert Betham.........................1746–1747
Samuel Quincy 1747–1749
Alexander Keith 1749–1753
John Andrews........................1755–1756
Robert Smith (First Bishop of So. Ca.).........1756–1759
Joseph D. Wilton 1761–1767
James Crallan 1767–1768
Robert Purcell 1769–1775
Thomas Frost 1786–1801
Peter M. Parker 1801–1802
Milward Pogson ....1802–....
James Dewar Simons .... –1809
Christopher E. Gadsden (Bishop) 1809–1814
Thomas D. Frost 1815–1819

There is probably no cemetery in this country which contains the remains of so many men who have been illustrious in its history, in Church and State, as does the Church Yard of St. Philip's. In this respect among others St. Philip's is the Abbey of South Carolina. Before the old church was completed Robert Daniel, who had been Deputy Governor of North Carolina, and a Landgrave and Governor of South Carolina, was buried near its rising walls, in 1718; and near him, about the same time, was interred George Logan, Speaker of the Commons. Still before the old church was opened Colonel William Rhett, the hero of the defense against the invasion of the Spaniards and French in 1706 and of the expedition against the pirates in 1718, the donor of the Silver Communion Service to the church,* was interred in the western yard, just in front of the church, in 1722. Thomas Hepworth, Chief Justice, was buried there in 1728. A slab of slate still marks the grave of the Rev. John Lambert, Master of the Free School and Afternoon Lecturer of the Parish, who died in 1729. In 1735 "the good Governor Robert Johnson," as he was affectionately called—Governor both under the Proprietary and Royal Governments—was interred near the chancel of the church. The profound jurist and

*Noble benefactions have from the earliest times been made to the church. Among the donors have been Mrs. Affra Coming—Colonel William Rhett—Mrs. Kirland—Mrs. Sarah Hort—Colin Campbell—James T. Welsman—Charles T. Lowndes—John Wroughton Mitchell, and his son Clarence G. Mitchell and grand-son Clarence B. Mitchell—Mrs. Juliet F. Wallace—Mrs. Harriet L. Gervais—Miss Susan B. Hayne—and Mrs. Anna D. Kaufman.

learned theologian, the father of the law and of the Courts in South Carolina, though, alas! the corrupt judge, Chief Justice Trott, worshipped in the church, and was buried in the church yard in 1740. Then followed three other Chief Justices—James Graeme, in 1752; Charles Pinckney, in 1758; and Peter Leigh, in 1759: and Andrew Rutledge, Speaker of the Commons, in 1755. The Rev. Alexander Garden, Commissary of the Bishop of London, was interred on the south side of the church in a tomb which the Vestry had built as a mark of their gratitude for his long and faithful services. To Hector Berenger DeBeaufain, Collector of Her Majesty's Customs, was erected a handsome memorial tablet in the old church by his fellow-citizens of the Province. Upon the walls of the old church stood also a slab to the memory of the Honorable Othniel Beale, a member of the King's Council, and for twenty-seven years Colonel of the Charlestown Regiment. Roger Pinckney, the last Royal Provost Marshal of the province, is buried in the eastern cemetery. The tomb of Benjamin Smith, Speaker from 1754 to 1764, still stands next to that of Colonel Rhett, his ancestor, in the western cemetery, directly in front of the church. Of physicians there worshipped in this church the two Doctors John Moultrie, father and son—Dr. John Rutledge, father of the distinguished trio of sons—and Dr. Lionel Chalmers: the two last are buried in the church yard.

Of the statesmen, heroes and exiles of the Revolution many lie around the edifice. Among these are Christopher Gadsden, the foremost of all, and William Johnson, his uncompromising follower and " right hand man;" Rawlins Lowndes, Governor in 1778, who requested that the epitaph upon his tomb should be: "The opponent of the adoption of the Constitution of the United States;" Edward Rutledge, signer of the Declaration of Independence and Governor; Colonel Isaac Motte, second in command at the battle of Fort Moultrie, 28th June, 1776; Thomas Pinckney, Major in the Continental Army during the Revolution, Major-General in the War of 1812, Minister to England and Spain, and Governor of the State; Major Benjamin Huger, who fell before the lines of Charlestown, on the 11th May, 1779, during Provost's invasion; Major Thomas Grimball, who commanded the Battalion of Artillery during the siege of Charlestown, in 1780; Daniel Huger, Charles Pinckney and John Lewis Gervais, the three members of the Council who accompanied Governor Rutledge when it was determined that he should leave the town before its surrender to the British, in order to preserve the Government of the State.

The Rev. Robert Smith, Rector of the Church and *first* Bishop of South Carolina, who was banished by the British authorities and his property confiscated, lies to the east of the church near the chancel.

Upon the walls of the old church there was a tablet to the memory of Jacob and Rebecca Motte. Jacob Motte was a distinguished citizen, long the Treasurer of the Province; his widow, Rebecca, was the heroine of Fort Motte, the lady who fired her own roof as the most decisive method of reducing the hostile British garrison which held and surrounded it with their works.

There was also a monument to the memory of Charles Dewar Simons, Professor of Natural Science and Chemistry in the South Carolina College, who was drowned near Columbia in 1812.

Of a later period are found the graves of Thomas W. Bacot the first Postmaster of Charleston under the present Constitution of the United States, who was appointed by Washington and held the office for forty-three years continuously; and of his son of the same name, Assistant Postmaster for thirty-six years under his father and the Hon. Alfred Huger; and also of Judge Elihu Hall Bay; Judge Theodore Gaillard; the "gifted" and brilliant William Crafts; the venerable Daniel Huger; Dr. Henry R. Frost, and Dr. Thomas G. Prioleau, chairmen of the Vestry; the distinguished son and grandsons of Bishop Smith, William Mason Smith, and J. J. Pringle Smith and William Mason Smith, Jr., the two former each for years Chairman of the Vestry; Mr. J. J. Pringle Smith, a distinguished representative of the Parish in the Diocesan Convention and of the Diocese in the General Convention of the Church, and a member of the Secession Convention; Henry D. Lesesne, Chairman of the Vestry, and a Chancellor of the State; and the late Charles Richardson Miles, Attorney-General of the State, and a delegate to the Diocesan Convention. John Blake White, the artist, and his son, Colonel Alonzo J. White, are buried in the eastern cemetery. Edward B. White, the architect, the builder of the present steeple, another son of the artist, a member of the church, is buried elsewhere.

The congregation has also furnished a number of distinguished Naval Officers. Col. Thomas Shubrick of the Revolution, himself the captain of a vessel—his four sons, Rear Admiral William Branford Shubrick, Captain John Taylor Shubrick who was lost at sea while bearing to the United States the treaty with Algiers in 1815, Captain Edward Rutledge Shubrick and Commodore Irwine Shubrick were all of this church.

A monumental stone, erected by the officers, seamen and marines of the United States Frigate Columbia, in memory of their beloved Commander Edward R. Shubrick, stands over his grave in the eastern church yard.

Commodore Duncan N. Ingraham of "Kosta" fame was for years chairman of the Vestry.

Within a hundred yards of each other, in the western cemetery of the church, it so happens that there lie, almost in line, the remains of four of the leaders of the great nullification struggle—on the one side the two *nullifiers* John C. Calhoun and Robert J. Turnbull—and on the other the two Johnsons, *union* men, sons of William, before mentioned, to wit, William Johnson, who was Speaker of the State House of Representatives at twenty-six years of age, a Judge on the State Bench at twenty-eight, and a Justice of the Supreme Court of the United States at thirty-two; and his brother, Dr. Joseph Johnson, Mayor of the city, etc.

The following deceased Members of Congress have come from the congregation: William Laughton Smith, General

John Rutledge, Joel R. Poinsett, William Lowndes, Henry
L. Pinckney, Isaac E. Holmes and William Aiken. William
Porcher Miles, still living, also a member of the congrega-
tion, was the last Member of Congress from the Charleston
District before the war, and was also a member of the Con-
federate Congress. It is remarkable that three Members of
Congress from Charleston were chosen in succession from
St. Philip's congregation, to wit : Holmes, Aiken and
Miles. The Hon. William Henry Trescot (still living), As-
sistant Secretary of State under President Buchanan's Ad-
ministration, Agent of the United States before the Halifax
Commission, Minister to China and to Peru, is also of this
church.

Besides the clergymen we have already named as buried
in the yard, there lie around the church : Bishop Smith,
Bishop Gadsden, Bishop Howe, the Reverends Thomas
Frost, Milward Pogson, James Dewar Simons, Thomas D.
Frost, Cranmore Wallace, Paul T. Gervais, Christopher P.
Gadsden, William Dehon, F. Marion Hall and James W.
Miles.

In the western church yard, besides Edward McCrady,
(one of the exiles and the first of his name in this country,)
above mentioned, there lie his son John, a brilliant young
lawyer, whose premature death was mourned by the community ; his son, the late venerable Edward McCrady,
lawyer and theologian, for years District Attorney of the
United States, and a member of the Secession Convention,
and who for over fifty years represented St. Philip's in the
Diocesan Convention, and for forty years was a member of
the Standing Committee of the Diocese, and for more than
thirty a Deputy of the Diocese in the General Convention of
the Episcopal Church ; and his sons—Professor John Mc-
Crady, Major of Engineers in the Confederate Army, Professor of Mathematics in the Charleston College, of Zoology
in Harvard, Cambridge, Mass., and of Biology in the University of the South—and Thomas McCrady, an officer of
the Confederate Army, and beloved by the community.
In this yard there is the grave of Colonel John DeBerniere,

of the British Army, the ancestor of several families in North and South Carolina.

In the eastern cemetery there is a slab with the simple inscription : " Mrs. Cornelia Fremont." This slab marks the grave of the mother of General John C. Fremont, the "Path Finder" across the Rocky Mountains, the first candidate of the Republican party for the Presidency of the United States, and Federal General in the late war.

Of others distinguished in the annals of the Province and State who worshipped in the Church, but were buried elsewhere, there were Sir Nathaniel Johnson, the Governor, under whose administration the invasion of the Province by the French and Spaniards took place in 1706, and the fierce contest was raged over the Church Acts of 1704-1706 ; the Rev. Gideon Johnson, Commissary, who was drowned in the harbor in 1716; Chief Justices Benjamin Whitaker and James Michie ; Arthur Middleton, President of the Convention which overthrew the Proprietary Government ; Henry Middleton, who was President of the Continental Congress in 1774; his son, Arthur Middleton, signer of the Declaration of Independence; his son, Henry Middleton, Governor of the State and Minister to Russia; Henry Laurens, President of the Continental Congress from 1776 to 1778 ; and his son, Col. John Laurens, an Aide to Washington and Envoy to France ; General William Moultrie, the hero of the 28th June, 1776, who twice saved the city from capture by the British ; Gabriel Manigault, for many years a Vestryman, who supported the Congress of the United States during the Revolution with a loan of $220,000; his son, Peter Manigault, Speaker of the Commons during the first Non-importation Movement; his grandsons, Edward Manigault, a Major in the United States Army during the Mexican war and Colonel in the Confederate service, and Arthur M. Manigault, also an officer in the Mexican war and Brigadier General in the Confederate service during the late war ; Isaac Mazyck, the great merchant—and his son of the same name, an Assistant Judge ; the wise and noble William Wragg, who exiled from his country because of his loyalty to his King, perished at sea, to whose memory there is a tablet in Westminster Abbey; Charles Cotesworth Pinckney, General in the Continental Army, member of the Convention which framed the Constitution of the United States, and Minister to France, long a Vestryman of the Church; Charles Pinckney, cousin of the last named, one of the exiles to St. Augustine, member of the Convention which framed the Constitution of the United States, United States Senator, Minister to Spain and Governor of the State ; Ralph Izard, a diplomat of the Revolution, member of the Continental Congress, and Senator of the United States; and his son, George, Major General in the War of 1812; Joel R. Poinsett, Secretary of War and Minister to Mexico; General James Gadsden, an officer of distinction in the War of 1812, and Minister to Mexico ; William Lowndes, of whom, it was said, the highest and best hopes of the country looked to him for their fulfillment, and whose character has been described by an eminent writer "as the ablest, purest and most unselfish statesman of his day," who died at sea; Francis H. Rutledge, the first Bishop of Florida ; Charles T. Lowndes, the eminent citizen and generous benefactor of the Church ; N. Russell Middleton, President of the Charleston College ; Isaac Hayne, for many years Attorney General of the State ; William Alston Pringle, Recorder of the city ; and Hon. Henry Buist, the distinguished lawyer.

The necrology of St. Philip's is thus rich in its material. Of the dignitaries of the Church in the line of the Episcopate there lie around her hallowed walls two Commissaries of the Bishop of London, three Bishops of the American Church, and seven ministers who have served at her altar. Of chief magistrates, two Colonial and three State Governors are buried within her precincts, besides numbering among her worshippers two other Colonial and four other State Governors who are buried elsewhere. Six Colonial Chief Justices worshipped in her sanctuary, four of whom are buried in her cemetery. Two Presidents of the Conti-

nental Congress and two signers of the Declaration of Independence were reared in this Church, one of the signers
resting near her walls. Ambassadors and ministers have gone
from her to foreign lands, and Members of Congress have
been again and again chosen from her members. Soldiers
of all the wars in which South Carolina, Province and State,
has been engaged lie within her gates. And there also are to
be found the graves of men of science. It is believed that
she has never been without a representation in the Senate or
House of the State Legislature.

All of the young men of the Church went at once into
the service of the Confederate States during the late war,
and in the vestibule there is placed this memorial of those
of them who gave their lives for their country:

IN MEMORY OF

THOSE SOLDIERS OF THE CONFEDERATE STATES

CONNECTED WITH ST. PHILIP'S CHURCH,

WHO DIED FOR THEIR COUNTRY.

HENRY AUGUSTUS MIDDLETON, JR,,
Co. A, Hampton Legion; mortally wounded Manassas, Va.,
21 July, 1861.
Died 27 July, 1861. Aged 31 years.

J. E. McPHERSON WASHINGTON,
1st Lieut., A. D. C. to Brig.-Gen. Garnett.
Died Montery, Va., 25 Aug., 1861. Aged 24 years.

EDMUND SHUBRICK HAYNE,
Co. L, 1 S. C. Vols.; mortally wounded Cold Harbour,Va., 27 June, 1862.
Died 30 June, 1862. Aged 18 years.

ALFRED GAILLARD PINCKNEY,
Co. L, 1 S. C. Vols.; killed Cold Harbour, Va., 27 June, 1862.
Aged 19 years.

ROBERT WOODWARD RHETT,
1st Lieut. Co. L, 1 S. C. Vols.; mortally wounded Cold Harbour, Va.,
27 June, 1862.
Died 30 June, 1862. Aged 23 years.

WILLIAM PRITCHARD,
Co. A, 25 S. C. Vols.
Died James Island, S. C., 16 Aug., 1862. Aged 30 years.

NATHANIEL HEYWARD, Jr.,
Co. L, 1 S. C. Vols.; killed Manassas, Va., 29 Aug., 1862.
Aged 19 years,

HARRY P. ROUX,
Co. A, Hampton Legion; killed Manassas, Va., 30 Aug., 1862.
Aged 19 years.

HENRY WRIGHT KINLOCH,
1st Lieut. Co. D, 6 S. C. Cav.
Died Aiken, S. C., 24 Oct., 1862.   Aged 30 years.

JOSEPH HEYWARD,
Capt. A. A. G. Provisional Army C. S.
Died 7 Novr., 1862.   Aged 32 years.

WASHINGTON ALSTON,
Sergt. Co. L, 1 S. C. Vols.; killed Fredricksburg, Va., 13 Dec., 1862.
Aged 18 years.

GEORGE COFFIN PINCKNEY,
Co. L, 1 S. C. Vols.; killed Fredricksburg, Va., 13 Dec., 1862.
Aged 25 years.

WILLIAM GAILLARD INGRAHAM,
Lieut. Co. B, Act'g. Adj't., 23 S. C. Vols.
Died 8 March, 1863.   Aged 22 years.

JOSEPH SANFORD FERGUSON,
Marion Art'y.
Died 15 July, 1863.   Aged 19 years.

WALTER EWING GIBSON,
Co. A, 25 S. C. Vols.; killed Fort Sumter, 31 Oct., 1863.
Aged 18 years.

JOHN WEBB,
Capt. Co. K, 2 S. C. Vols.; killed Spottsylvania, Va., 12 May, 1864.
Aged 26 years.

JAMES MERRITT SCHMIDT,
Co. C, 11 S. C. Vols.; killed Drewry's Bluff, Va., 16 May, 1864.
Aged 31 years.

FRANCIS KINLOCH MIDDLETON,
Co. K, 4 S. C. Cav.; mortally wounded Hawes Shop, Va., 28 May, 1864.
Died 30 May, 1864.   Aged 29 years.

CHARLES EDWARD PRIOLEAU,
Co. K, 4 S. C. Cav.; killed Hawes Shop, Va., 28 May, 1864.
Aged 24 years.

WILLIAM HUEY FAIRLEY,
Co. K, 4 S. C. Cav.; killed Trevillian's Sta., Va., 11 June, 1864.
Aged 27 years.

WILLIAM MASON SMITH,
1st Lieut., Adj't. 27 S. C. Vols.; mortally wounded Cold Harbour, Va.,
3 June, 1864.
Died Richmond, Va., 16 Aug., 1864.   Aged 21 years.

MATTHEW VASSAR BANCROFT,
Major 23 S. C. Vols.; killed Petersburg, Va., 22 June, 1864.
Aged 25 years.

ISAAC BALL GIBBS,
Co. B, 25 S. C. Vols.; killed Reams Sta., Va., 21 Aug., 1864.
Aged 23 years.

JACOB JOHN GUERARD,
1st Lieut. Co. C, 11 S. C. Vols.; died in prison Fort Delaware, 14 Sept.,
1864.
Aged 33 years.

EDWARD B. HEYWARD,
Marion Art'y.; died Church Flats, S. C., 6 Dec., 1864.
Aged 24 years.

PETER MANIGAULT,
Co. H, 3 S. C. Cav.; killed Ball's Ferry, Oconee River, Ga.,
23 Nov., 1864.
Aged 59 years.

ALFRED MANIGAULT,
Co. K, 4 S. C. Cav.; died Winnsboro, S. C., 20 Feb'y, 1865.
Aged 24 years.

HENRY RUSSELL LESESNE,
Capt. Co. H, 1 S. C. Regular Art'y.; killed Averysboro, N. C.,
16 March, 1865.
Aged 22 years.

BURGH SMITH BURNET,
Capt. Co. F, 1 S. C. Regular Inf'y.; mortally wounded Averysboro, N. C.
16 March, 1865.
Died 28 March, 1865.   Aged 28 years.

FRANCIS KINLOCH LESESNE,
Marion Art'y.; died 24 June, 1865.   Aged 20 years.

www.ingramcontent.com/pod-product-compliance
Lightning Source LLC
Chambersburg PA
CBHW031746090426
42739CB00008B/904